THE
RUMI
DAYBOOK

SELECTED AND TRANSLATED BY

Kabir & Camille Helminski

SHAMBHALA
Boston & London
2012

Shambhala Publications, Inc.
Horticultural Hall
300 Massachusetts Avenue
Boston, Massachusetts 02115
www.shambhala.com

9 8 7 6 5 4 3 2 1

First Edition
Printed in the United States of America

∞ This edition is printed on acid-free paper that meets
the American National Standards Institute z39.48 Standard.
♻ Shambhala Publications makes every effort to print on recycled paper.
For more information please visit www.shambhala.com.
Distributed in the United States by Random House, Inc.,
and in Canada by Random House of Canada Ltd

Designed by Lora Zorian

Library of Congress Cataloging-in-Publication Data
Jalal al-Din Rumi, Maulana, 1207–1273.
[Masnavi. English. Selections]
The Rumi daybook / selected and translated
by Kabir Helminski and Camille Helminski.
p.   cm.
Poems.
Translated from Persian.
Includes bibliographical references.
ISBN 978-1-59030-894-3 (pbk.: alk. paper)
I. Helminski, Kabir Edmund, 1947– II. Helminski, Camille Adams, 1951–
III. Title.
PK6481.M8E52 2012
891'.5511—dc22
2011014499

CONTENTS

PREFACE

In the Name of our Infinitely Compassionate and Infinitely Merciful Source

Speech is of three kinds: the first comes from the desire of the self, the second from reason, and the third from love. Speech which arises from desire is troubling and insipid, giving neither pleasure to those who speak nor profit to those who listen. That which arises from reason is accepted by the wise and gives pleasure to the listener and the speaker, and speech that arises from love renders enraptured those who listen and those who speak.*

FOR OVER THIRTY-FIVE YEARS NOW we have been following the Way of Rumi, so grateful for his companionship, his heart, his being and example, grateful to be allowed the moments to immerse in his loving words and his presence and that of his mentor and dearest friend, Shams of Tabriz. And we are grateful to be able to share with you now this small offering of passages from Rumi's overflowing fountain of deep heart wisdom. We've

---

* *Menaqib al-Arifin*, passage 414, excerpted from *Rumi and His Friends, Stories of the Wise,* selections from Aflaki, translated by Camille Helminski and Susan Blaylock.

chosen to open this volume with the selection "You Are Joy," offering that as the context for the unfolding of this daybook, because the recognition of the joy that opens from the speech of Love feels so needed in our world at this time. Many challenges face us in current times, but Rumi also lived in the midst of very challenging times. Still he was able continually to open to and rely on that deeper joy of Love, moving through every moment and every manifestation. His words assist us in discovering that love within ourselves and among us all, sustaining all that is.

In a passage from the *Menaqib al-Arifin*, the "Stories of the Wise Ones," of the spiritual path that unfolded following the example of Rumi, his son Sultan Weled relates the following story:

> Sultan Weled told us this: One day I felt bored and downhearted. My father came into the college and saw that I was sad and said: "Are you angry at someone? You seem so downcast."
>
> "I don't really know what the matter is," I replied.
>
> He disappeared into another room and, after a few minutes, returned with his face and head covered with an old wolfskin.
>
> "Bou! Bou!" he cried, just as if I were a child again.
>
> I burst out laughing and laughed until I could laugh no more and then kissed my father's blessed feet.
>
> "Oh, Bahaeddin," he said. "Are you afraid when someone who loves you dresses up in a wolfskin?"
>
> "No," I said.
>
> "That same person who can cause you such joy can also cause you sorrow.

Why feel sad for no good reason
and why allow yourself to be a prisoner of negativity?
Find a way out of your despondency,
and know that all difficulties have a common cause.
Treat your joy like a delicate plant and water it;
when it has borne fruit share that with your friends."

"As my father spoke," Sultan Weled continued, "I experienced a profound feeling of ecstasy and my heart expanded like a flower. For the rest of my life, I never again felt sad and learned to detach from the troubles of the world."*

It is always a joy to share the encouraging words of Rumi with others and feel hearts awakening to that friendship—and through him, friendship with the Beloved, the Source of all our sustenance and growth and well-being, no matter what experience we may be passing through at any moment. Continually Rumi's words convey to us the fragrance of that placeless place of Love, calling us into the Presence of the Beloved. May we keep opening more and more to that Presence and that Love:

It is Love that makes people happy.
It is Love that fills happiness with joy.
It is Love that birthed me, not my mother.
A hundred blessings and praises to that Mother!

Your fragrance is always with me.
Your Face never leaves my sight.

---

* Ibid., passage 209.

Day and night I've been longing for You.
My life is spent, but my desire for You remains.

O heart, throw your clothes down upon the way,
and cover your face with the shirt of Joseph.
You're just a small fish; you can't live without water.
Don't think about it, just throw yourself into this stream.*

—*Camille Helminski*

* Mevlana Jalaluddin Rumi: Quatrain 449, Quatrain 450, and Quatrain 936. Translated by Camille and Kabir Helminski. The numbering of the quatrains is according to the numbering used by Mr. Badi' al-Zaman Faruzanfar in his edition of the *Divan-e Shams-e Tabrizi*.

INTRODUCTION

BEFORE BEGINNING to read this collection of Rumi's writings one would do well to have some sense of the spiritual universe he came from—the culture of mystical Islam that flourished in the Persian-speaking lands from Anatolia to Khorasan, that is, the lands from central Turkey east as far as northwestern Iran, Afghanistan, and Central Asia.

Mystical Islam was at that time a respected, almost mainstream phenomenon, characterized by an abiding sense of the sacred, an appreciation of the dignity of the human being, and a high degree of spiritual refinement. The Qur'an asserts that Adam, the archetypal human being, was uniquely endowed by God with an understanding of the Divine Names—that is, the fundamental components of reality. Everything in the manifest world is comprised of its own proportions of these divine attributes. To see the world in this way is to see through appearances and recognize an underlying spiritual reality that gives birth to it all.

As it is said in the Qur'an, God has *"honored the children of Adam,"* * and each human being has the inherent capacity to know the whole of reality and experience the immense dimensions of Divine Love.

The Sufis, or mystics of Islam, carried this notion even further, committing themselves to spiritual practices to harmonize

---

* *Surah al-Isra'* (The Night Journey), [17:70]. Throughout this volume, passages from the Qur'an are rendered in italic.

their wills with the Divine Will, or, to express it more unequivocally, to die to the imaginary ego and live through Divine Intelligence. Rumi says: "I have found true being in non-being, so I wove my selfhood into nothingness."* The subject of becoming nothing is a subtle one and easily misunderstood. It is not the denial or suppression of our individuality; it certainly didn't stifle Rumi's creativity to lose himself and be overwhelmed by the Divine. Rather it is to pass from a superficial identity constructed of social conditioning and random desires, and to begin to live from something deeper, a sense of self without an "I," but a self that lives through a greater intelligence and being.

Whatever the ultimate nature of reality, and the metaphysics that describes it, there is also a practical teaching here, often embedded in very human stories, striking metaphors, and earthy humor. Some of what you will find in these pages is practical advice for reducing our egoism and cultivating human character: "Vain breathings and lies can't be joined with truth. O brother, you are what you think. As for the rest of you, it's only flesh and bone. If your thought is a rose, you are a rose garden; and if your thoughts are thorns, you are just kindling for the bath-stove."†

There is, as well, much in these pages that helps us to accept and even benefit from the sufferings of life, and to meet the inevitable tests of life with courage and trust: "How will the bread be baked if the wheat is not milled? How can uncrushed grapes yield wine?" These are teachings that instill trust and awaken us to the knowledge that Divine Mercy reigns in the end. "Only He has the right to destroy who knows how to rebuild better than before."

In addition there are teachings that help us to recognize our need for a transcendent reality, especially when, in our own shame,

---

* *Mathnawi* I: 1735.

† *Mathnawi* II: 277–278.

we want to turn and run away into the oblivion of separation: "Water says to the dirty, 'Come.' But the dirty one says, 'But I'm so ashamed.' Water says, 'But how will you become clean without me?'"

Other assertions in this daybook might be bewildering to people who are unacquainted with some of the deeper metaphysical principles that were current in Rumi's spiritual milieu. One of the important themes in Rumi's universe is the metaphysical notion that what is most real is beyond appearances and forms, yet perceptible to the purified heart.

The human heart has the capacity to directly perceive the spiritual nature of reality, to witness the qualities and signs of God in the theater of manifest life, and yet too often we chase after shadows that have no real substance. We have an itch and a restlessness we do not know how to satisfy. Underneath all our forms of restlessness and desiring is a yearning that is precious, but when we scatter ourselves we betray and abandon that yearning.

All forms spring from formless spirit, as speech from thought, as waves from the sea, but to be too attached to these forms is a kind of idolatry. While this world is full of Divine gifts, our focus should not be primarily on the gifts but on the Giver of the gifts.

Spiritual perception involves seeing things as they really are, less from our egoic perspective and more from a vision of unity. Spiritual knowledge is like a light that can pierce through all the levels of reality. It is different from worldly knowledge, which can become a veil over the eye of the heart or a useless burden to be carried by a faulty memory. With spiritual knowledge we can know and feel the generosity that is at the heart of reality. With even a slight glimpse of this reality we may become motivated to cleanse our hearts and minds of the ego's distortions, finally to experience a knowledge that wells up and flows from a spring within the heart. "Consult your heart," is Rumi's continual advice, and if the heart is pure it will lead you to the highest spiritual truth.

Let's consider the following quatrain, which could not be adequately understood without taking into account the deep metaphysics that underlies its assertions:

O you who study the world, you're just a hired worker.
And you who want Paradise, you're far from the Truth.
And you who are happy with the two worlds, but unaware,
because you have not experienced the happiness of His
    sorrow,
you're simply excused.

Divan-e Shams-e Tabrizi: Quatrain 1784

Here he is telling us that the work of intellectuals and scientists who direct their whole attention to merely studying the outer world are no more than "hired workers." This could also apply to those who intellectualize the spiritual journey without emptying themselves of desires, quieting the mind, and stilling the emotions so as to directly experience the Divine Presence.

And those who engage in religious activities out of a desire for earning Paradise are far from the Truth of experiencing the Divine here and now through the finer perception of the heart. For such people, spirituality is just another strategy to allow the ego to feel superior; whereas the realization of Truth is the realization of one's essential nothingness before the Face of God.

And those who live a happy but superficial life and have not found the blessing and meaning that can come with the inevitable sufferings of life are not at the same level of spiritual maturity as those who experience "the happiness of His sorrow." For the person living in the fullness of his spiritual being, nothing is a misfortune.

One of the most powerful themes in Rumi's writing is transformation. As he says:

That which God said to the rose,
And caused it to laugh in full-blown beauty,
He said to my heart,
And made it a hundred times more beautiful.*

Perhaps nowhere else in literature are the possibilities of transformation illustrated more explicitly or more beautifully. The agent of transformation is Divine Love: "By love the bitter becomes sweet; copper becomes gold; the king becomes a slave." The Divine is "an explosive force causing our dammed up rivers to burst forth."

And nothing is more valuable or has a greater capacity for transformation than the human being. Our humanness has been given to us for this purpose. We are here to do the work of the prophets and saints. The work of love is the supreme work. It is like "a golden bowl, not to be used just for boiling turnips."†

The ultimate purpose of life is fulfilled in the mature human being: "Beyond the body, life, and soul is the dervish. Better than earth and sky is the dervish. God's purpose was not to create these worlds, but the purpose of these worlds is the dervish."‡ Saints are the Intellect of the intellect. The "person of heart" is the All.

Rumi experienced this transformation through his relationship with Shams of Tabriz, the intimate friend who reflected the Divine Friend. Sometimes Rumi addresses this friend as "You," long predating Martin Buber's *I and Thou* (1924). Rumi was drunk with the joy of being in relationship with the ultimate Beloved, the Source of our Being. This relationship is not an abstract and

---

* *Mathnawi* III: 4, 129. From *Jewels of Remembrance*, translated by Camille and Kabir Helminski, 1996

† *Fihi ma Fihi*: Discourse 3.

‡ *Divan-e Shams-e Tabrizi*: Quatrain 255.

impersonal relationship; rather it is the kind of relationship that can be profoundly transformative if we welcome it. The human being can become the lover of the Divine Beloved and equally the beloved of God. Free will is the effort to thank the Divine for Its gifts.

A fundamental theme of Islamic mysticism is this: *"If it weren't for you (O Human Being), I (God) would not have created the worlds."* Everything beautiful is made for the eye of one who sees, and the human being has an extraordinary potential for vision. The universe was created by Infinite Divine Generosity for satisfying needs, but we have often allowed our needs to be too trivial and vulgar. Everything is given according to need. A mole in the ground is given just the faculties it needs and no more. We should, therefore, cultivate a noble and grand need so that the Divine could have the pleasure of fulfilling such a need. "Abundance is seeking beggars, just as beauty seeks a mirror; beggars, then, are the mirrors of God's bounty."* We are all beggars before God's abundance.

The only phenomenon that could not be completely and adequately explained in Rumi's cosmology is Love. As he says: "When the discourse reached the topic of Love the tip of my pen broke. If intellect tries to explain it, it falls helpless as a donkey on a muddy trail. Only Love itself can explain Love and the mystery of being a lover."†

But I hope our humble efforts in this book can lead you to the shore of that Ocean of Love.

Someone asked, "What is love?" I answered,
"You will know when you become 'we.'"

Mathnawi II: Prologue.

—*Kabir Helminski*

---

* *Mathnawi* I: 2745, 2750. From *Rumi Daylight*, translated by Camille and Kabir Helminski, 1990.
† Ibid., *Mathnawi* I: 114–115.

A NOTE ON THESE TRANSLATIONS

WE HAVE BEEN TRANSLATING Rumi's work since 1977, and my first book of translations, *The Ruins of the Heart,* was published in 1980. In all these years we have made use of reliable literal translations as well as collaborations with colleagues whose first language is Farsi. While we have the ability to read the Farsi and make judgments on how to translate certain vocabulary, especially the spiritual terminology, what we bring to the table is less linguistic expertise and more a sense of the poetic possibilities of contemporary English and an awareness of the spiritual context of Rumi's words.

In this book we have taken more liberties than before in order to present Rumi's meanings in a way that will touch the hearts and minds of readers of contemporary English. But the liberties we take are more in the form of the poems than in the content. Let me give an example of what I mean. Consider this literal translation by Reynold A. Nicholson:

> The bird is flying on high, and its shadow is speeding on
>   the earth, flying like a bird:
> Some fool begins to chase the shadow, running (after it)
>   so far that he becomes powerless (exhausted),
> Not knowing that it is the reflexion of that bird in the
>   air, not knowing where is the origin of the shadow.
>
> He shoots arrows at the shadow; his quiver is emptied
>   in seeking (to shoot it):

The quiver of his life became empty: his life passed in
    running hotly in chase of the shadow.
(But) when the shadow of God is his nurse, it delivers
    him from (every) phantom and shadow.
The shadow of God is that servant of God who is dead
    to this world and living through God.*

Now see how we have presented the same lines.

Of Shadows and Saints

A bird is flying high;
its shadow speeds over the earth like an actual bird:

a fool starts to chase the shadow,
running so far that he exhausts himself,
not knowing that it is but the reflection of that bird in the air,
not knowing where the origin of the shadow is.

He shoots arrows at the shadow and the quiver is emptied—
his life is wasted by what he seeks.
But when the shadow of God tends to him,
it saves him from every illusion.

The shadow of God is that servant of God
who has died to this world and is living through that One.

It would, of course, be unfair to judge Nicholson on the basis
of poetic criteria when his intention was to accurately translate
every word from Rumi so that a student could go through it along

---

* *Mathnawi* I: 417–423.

with a Persian text and make sense of it. We owe to him a great debt. But the need we are trying to serve is the need for intelligibility and faithfulness to the sprit of Rumi. You will notice that we have given the selection a title that it did not originally have, and we have broken the lines according to the conventions of contemporary free verse. It is hoped that our version can be more directly understood and yet will have some of the qualities of good poetry: imagery, rhythm, allusiveness, economy. My favorite portion of the poem is:

> He shoots arrows at the shadow and the quiver is emptied—
> his life is wasted by what he seeks. [nine syllables],
> But when the shadow of God tends to him,
> it saves him from every illusion. [nine syllables]

Even though these lines are not exactly what Rumi said as translated by Nicholson: "his life passed in running hotly in chase of the shadow" (fourteen syllables), it has an economy that is echoed in the nine-syllable line that follows shortly: "it saves him from every illusion."

There are countless calculations, most of them immediate and spontaneous, that enter into the judgment of how to translate lines from Rumi. Meaning, of course, is foremost, with an intuitive sense of sound not far behind, and there is also an awareness of the whole metaphysical background of Sufism. This selection is particularly exemplary of the way Rumi can convey sublime and nuanced metaphysical concepts in unforgettable and easily graspable images and metaphors. If only we could see how we are wasting ourselves by chasing mere shadows reflected upon the earth.

We hope you enjoy and benefit from this work.

—*Kabir Helminski*

REFERENCE WORKS

Works we have relied upon and authors to whom we are indebted follow below. May God bless all their work. We wish to also thank Shambhala Publications staff, especially Dave O'Neal, Katie Keach, and Lora Zorian for their gracious help in completing this volume and making it available, and all the dear friends, too numerable to mention, whose hearts' yearning have pulled it into form. May God accept this offering, make it fruitful, and forgive our mistakes.

MATHNAWI

The Mathnawi of Jalalu'ddin Rumi, translated by Reynold A. Nicholson with Persian text. London: Luzac & Co. 1925, 1929, 1933 reprinted 1982 E. J. W. Gibb Memorial Trust, Cambridge, England.

FIHI MA FIHI (*"In It What Is in It"*)

Fihi ma Fihi (Farsi), Amir Kabir, Tehran, 1385 (AH).
Discourses of Rumi (translation of *Fihi ma Fihi*), by A. J. Arberry, John Murray, Ltd., London, 1961.
Signs of the Unseen (translation *of Fihi ma Fihi*), by Wheeler Thackston, Threshold Books, Putney, 1994.

DIVAN-E SHAMS (source for the quatrains)

Divan-e Shams-e Tabrizi, edited by Badi' al-Zaman Foruzanfar, Amir Kabir, Tehran, 1977.

The Quatrains of Rumi, by Ibrahim Gamard and Rawan Farhadi, Sufi Dari Books, San Rafael, 2008.
Rending the Veil, by Sharam T. Shiva, Hohm Press, 1995.

We also are grateful to Lida Saedian for her collaboration on the translation of some of the quatrains.

The Rumi Daybook

O my God, our intoxicated eyes have blurred our vision.
Our burdens have become heavy, forgive us.
You are hidden, and yet from East to West,
You have filled the world with Your radiance.
Your Light is more magnificent than sunrise or sunset,
and You are the inmost ground of consciousness
revealing the secrets we hold.
You are an explosive force
causing our damned-up rivers to burst forth.
You whose essence is hidden while Your gifts are manifest,
You are like water and we are like millstones.
You are like wind and we are like dust.
The wind is hidden while the dust is plainly seen.
You are the invisible spring, and we are Your lush garden.

You are the Spirit of life and we are like hand and foot.
Spirit causes the hand to close and open.
You are intelligence; we are Your voice.
Your intelligence causes this tongue to speak.
You are joy and we are laughter,
for we are the result of the blessing of Your joy.
All our movement is really a continual profession of faith,
bearing witness to Your eternal power,
just as the powerful turning of the millstone
professes faith in the river's existence.
Dust settles upon my head and upon my metaphors,
for You are beyond anything we can ever think or say.
And yet, this servant cannot stop trying to express Your beauty,
in every moment, let my soul be Your carpet.

[*Mathnawi* V: 3307–3319]

Dancing in the Breeze

The beloved shines like the sun;
the lover whirls like the planets.
When love's spring breeze blows,
every moist branch starts dancing.

[*Divan-e Shams-e Tabrizi:* Quatrain 466]

Only Love Can Explain Itself

Love is the astrolabe of God's mysteries.
A lover may be drawn to this love or that love,
but finally he is drawn to the Sultan of love.
However much we describe and explain love,
when we fall in love we are ashamed of our words.
Explanation by the tongue makes most things clear,
but love unexplained is clearer.

When the pen came to the subject of love, it broke.
When the discourse reached the topic of love,
the pen split and the paper tore.
If intellect tries to explain it,
it falls helpless as a donkey on a muddy trail;
only Love itself can explain love and lovers!
The proof of the sun is the sun itself.
If you wish to see it, don't turn away from it.

[*Mathnawi* I: 110–116]

THE HUMAN BEING is an astrolabe of God, but it takes an astronomer to know how to use the astrolabe. If a seller of onions or a grocer were to possess an astrolabe, what benefit could he get out of it? What would he understand of the circling heavens and the movements of the planets, their influences and transits?

In the hands of an astronomer the astrolabe is of good use, for "he who knows himself knows his Lord."* Just as this metal astrolabe is a mirror of the heavens, the human being—*and We have honored the children of Adam* [17:70]—is the astrolabe of God. When God makes a person to know himself, through the astrolabe of that person's own being he witnesses the manifestation of God and His infinite beauty moment by moment and flash by flash. That beauty is never absent from his "mirror."

[*Fihi ma Fihi*: Discourse 2]

---

* This is a *hadith*, a saying of the Prophet Muhammad, that is a favorite among the mystics: (*man 'arafa*) see Badi' (al-Zaman) Faruzanfar, *Ahadith al-Mathnawi*, p. 167.

If some refuse gets into the mouth of one who is alive,
he's disturbed until he spits it out.
When, among thousands of bits,
one trashy morsel enters,
the living one's sense discovers it.
Bodily senses are the ladder through this world;
spiritual perception is the ladder to Heaven.
From a doctor, seek the well-being of the former;
beg the well-being of spiritual insight
from your Beloved.

[*Mathnawi* I: 301–304]

The health of the senses of this world
comes from the well-being of the body;
the health of one's spiritual sense
arises from the body's ruin.

The spiritual path wrecks the body,
but afterward restores it to health:
it destroys the house to unearth the treasure,
then with that treasure builds it better than before.

The water is stopped and the riverbed cleansed,
so that purer water might flow.
The flesh is cut open to draw out the arrow—
so that fresh skin might heal the wound.

[*Mathnawi* I: 305–308]

Who could ever describe
the ways of the One who is like no other?
Anything I could say is only an attempt
at what might be needed now.

Sometimes God's movement appears one way—
and sometimes as its opposite.
The work of real religion is bewilderment;
but not a bewilderment that drives you away
from Him, no, but bewildered like this—
drowned and drunk with the Beloved.

One person's face is turned
toward the Beloved in awe,
another only faces himself.

Gaze upon each person's face.
Pay attention. Perhaps through service
you might come to know
the Face of the Beloved.

[*Mathnawi* I: 311–315]

"DON'T DESPAIR, for *none despairs of God's kindness, except the deniers* [12:87]."

My purpose in speaking was to help him understand, give alms and humble himself before God, for he had fallen to a low state from a very high state, but he should still be hopeful. God works in mysterious ways. Things may look beneficial outwardly, but there may be harm within them. Let no one be deluded by conceit that he himself has birthed good ideas or has done good deeds.

If everything were as it seemed, the Prophet would not have cried out with such illuminated and illuminating insight, "Show me things as they are!* You make things seem beautiful when in reality they are ugly; You make things seem ugly when in reality they are beautiful. Therefore, show us each thing as it is so that we might not fall into a trap and be really in error."

Now your judgment, however good, however clear it may be, is not better than Muhammad's, and he spoke as he did. Don't rely on your own thoughts and opinions, but humble yourself before God and stand in awe of Him.

[*Fihi ma Fihi*: Discourse 1]

---

* This hadith (*arinâ 'l-ashyâ . . .*) may be found in *FAM* 45, no. 116.

It was the era of Jesus and the turn was his:
He was the soul of Moses, and Moses the soul of him,
but the squinting king made it seem they were two,
those Messengers of God who really were as one.

A master said to a squinting student,
"Come here, and bring me that bottle."
Said the squint-eyed one: "Which of the bottles
shall I bring to you? Let me know."

"There aren't two bottles," said the master.
"Stop squinting, don't double them."
"O master," he said, "don't scold me."
The master replied, "All right, then smash one of them!"

The bottle was one; though to his eyes it seemed two,
and when he broke that bottle, nothing was left.
When one was broken, both vanished from sight.

Anger and lust make a man squint;
they cloud the spirit so it strays from truth.
When self-interest appears, virtue hides:
a hundred veils rise between the heart and the eye.

[*Mathnawi* I: 325–334]

No Prayer Is Complete without Presence

O God, what a good helper You are!
Hear and respond to the cry of those in difficulty.
O God, there are so many traps, so many baits,
and we are like hungry, greedy birds.
Every moment we're caught in some new snare,
even when we might become a falcon or bird of the heavens.*
O You who are without need, each moment You free us,
and then again we fall into another trap!

We put grain into our barn, and then lose it.
Why don't we consider that this loss
comes from the gnawing of mice?
These little mice have ruined our barn.
O soul, first stop the mischief of the mice;
then work to gather the grain.
Hear a saying of the Master of Masters:
"No prayer is complete without presence."†

If there is no thievish mouse in our barn,
where is the harvest of these forty years of devotion?
Why doesn't the sincerity of each day accumulate,
bit by bit, here in this barn?

[*Mathnawi* I: 373–384]

---

* The Simurgh is a majestic mythical bird capable of flying into the Divine Presence. See *The Conference of the Birds* by Farid ud-Din Attar.

† This is a hadith. "Presence" is the concentration of the mind on God. See *Living Presence: A Sufi Way to Mindfulness and the Essential Self* by Kabir Helminski (New York: Jeremy P. Tarcher, 1992).

This body of clay is the chalice of the heart.
My fermented thought is the heart's new wine.
The seed of knowledge is what captures the heart.
I talk about it, but the heart revealed it.

[*Divan-e Shams-e Tabrizi:* Quatrain 260]

Though a thousand snares catch our feet,
when You are with us there is no difficulty.
Every night You free spirits from the body's snare,
and clear the tablets of the mind.
Every night spirits are set free from this cage,
no longer ruled by rules or long stories.

At night prisoners have no sense of imprisonment,
at night governors are unconscious of their power.
There is no sorrow, no thought of gain or loss,
no tales of this person or another.
Even without sleep this is how the gnostic* is.
As God said, *You would think they were awake,*
while they slept.†

Have no doubt: there are those who are asleep,
day and night, to the affairs of this world,
yet moving like a pen in the hand of God.

[*Mathnawi* I: 387–394]

---

* The term translated as "gnostic" here is *'arif* (the spiritual knower).
† *Surah Kahf* (The Cave), [18:18].

A bird is flying high;
its shadow speeds over the earth like an actual bird.

A fool starts to chase the shadow,
running so far that he exhausts himself,
not knowing that it is but the reflection of that bird in the air,
not knowing where the origin of the shadow is.

He shoots arrows at the shadow and the quiver is emptied—
his life is wasted by what he seeks.
But when the shadow of God tends to him,
it saves him from every illusion.

The shadow of God is that servant of God
who has died to this world and is living through that One.
Quickly, take hold of his robe,
that you may be saved during the last days of this earth.

[*Mathnawi* I: 417–424]

SOMEONE ASKED, "Is there any better way to draw near to God than prayer?"

He answered, "More prayer, but not just the prayer of outer form—that is just the 'body' of prayer, because it has a beginning and an end. Anything that has a beginning and an end is a 'body.' Witnessing the greatness of God is the beginning of the formal prayer and the greeting of peace is its end. Likewise, there is more to the profession of faith than what is uttered with the tongue, because it, too, has a beginning and an end. Anything that can be expressed in words and has a beginning and an end is a 'form,' a 'body'; its 'body,' however, is formless and infinite, without beginning or end.

"Anyway, prayer as we know it was brought into form by the prophets. Now the Prophet Muhammad, who gave form to prayer, said, 'I have a "moment" with God during which there is no room for either message-bearing prophet or angel close to God to enter with me.'[*] We know then that the 'soul' of prayer is not only the outer form but also a state of complete absorption and unconsciousness during which all these external forms, for which there is no room, remain outside. In that state there is no place even for Gabriel, who is pure consciousness."

[*Fihi ma Fihi*: Discourse 3]

---

[*] This is a hadith (*li ma'a 'llah* ...). See *FAM* 39, 100. The reference to "moment" (*waqt*) is also understood to mean "state."

My Cure

My heart wandered through the world
constantly seeking after my cure,
but the sweet and delicious water of life
had to break through the granite of my heart.

[*Divan-e Shams-e Tabrizi:* Quatrain 1501]

Envy

If on the Way envy grabs you by the throat,
know it is Satan who goes to any lengths.
In his envy he despised Adam,
and out of envy is at war with happiness.

On the Way there is nothing harder than
giving up envy as your companion!
The body, you must know,
can become a house of envy,
completely besotted with envy.
Yet God can cleanse it.

The purified heart is a treasure of Light,
even though it has an earthy talisman.
But when you become so entangled
that you envy someone who has no envy himself,
your heart is stained black.
Become like dust under the feet of God's friends.
Throw dust on the head of envy, even as we do.

[*Mathnawi* I: 429–436]

How many a generous rain has poured,
so that the sea could scatter pearls!
How many a sun of blessing has shone,
so that clouds and seas might learn generosity!

The sunbeams of Wisdom struck the soil,
so that earth might receive seed:
the soil is faithful to its trust—
whatever you sow, you reap.

The soil's faithfulness comes from that Faithful One,
since the Sun of Justice shines on it.
Until springtime brings the touch of God,
the earth doesn't reveal her secrets.

[*Mathnawi* I: 501–511]

My Heart Smile

I'm blissfully unaware; only the God of Truth knows
what will make my heart smile.
That said, by the grace of the dawn breeze
petals are scattered from the heart's bough.

[*Divan-e Shams-e Tabrizi:* Quatrain 646]

When you fall ill, remorse and humility open;
the moment one falls ill, conscience awakens.
When you fall ill, you pray God to forgive your sins.
The murkiness of your error becomes apparent to you,
and you resolve to return to the Way.

You promise and vow that from now on you'll choose
nothing but obedience to God.
See how illness stirs your conscience and wakes you up.
So pay attention to this principle, O seeker;
anyone who suffers pain has caught the scent.

The more wakeful anyone is, the more he suffers;
the more spiritually aware he is, the paler is his face.
If you are aware of God's compelling,
where is your humility?
Where is your feeling of being bound by His Omnipotence?
How should one who is bound in chains dance?
Since when does the prisoner act like one who is free?
And if you see that your foot is shackled
and that the Sultan's officers are keeping watch over you,
don't act like a tyrant toward those who are helpless,
since that's not how helpless people act.

[*Mathnawi* I: 623–633]

In the Fire

O my heart, whenever like dust you let yourself be scattered,
you abandon my poor soul to its longing.
But now you're in the fire and I will leave you there.
Here's your last chance to become a master.

[*Divan-e Shams-e Tabrizi:* Quatrain 1922]

A KING SAID TO A DERVISH, "In the moment when you enter the glorious intimacy of God's court, mention me."

"When I am in that Presence," said the dervish, "and the Light of that Sun of Beauty shines on me, I am unable to remember myself—how shall I remember you!"

Yet even so, when God has chosen one of His servants and caused him to be completely absorbed in Himself, if anyone should grab hold of that person's robe asking him to make a request of God, God will grant that request without the mystic even mentioning his need to Him.

The story is told of a king who had a subject he held in high regard. When that person would set out for the king's palace, everyone who had a request to make would give him a letter describing their situation to present to the king, and he would put them all in a small bag. When he entered the king's presence and the king's radiant beauty completely overwhelmed him, he would fall unconscious at the king's feet. The king would then lovingly put his hand into the man's small bag, saying, "What has this amazed servant of mine who is so absorbed in my beauty?" He would take out the letters and write his approval on their backs and then return them to the bag. And so, without even being presented by His servant, all the requests were granted; not a single one was ever denied. On the contrary, the petitioners received much more than they asked for. However, when other servants who remained conscious brought petitions of those in need before the king, only now and then was one out of a hundred of those ever granted.

[*Fihi ma Fihi*: Discourse 3]

When God wants to tear someone's veil,
He inclines him toward speaking ill of holy ones.
When God wishes to cover our faults,
He keeps us from breathing even a word of blame.
When He wants to help us,
He bends us toward humble asking.
Heartache for His sake brings happiness.
Laughter will come after tears.
Whoever foresees this is a servant blessed by God.
Wherever water flows, life flourishes:
wherever tears fall, Divine Mercy appears.

[*Mathnawi* I: 815–820]

To those who know God
the wind of death is soft and pleasant
like the breeze that carries the fragrance of Joseph.

The fire didn't bite Abraham:
how should it, since he is God's chosen?
The faithful weren't burned by the fire of lust
that took so many down into the bowels of earth.

The waves of the sea, moved by God's command,
could distinguish the people of Moses from those of Pharoah.

When the Divine command came,
the earth sucked Midas down into darkness
with his throne and all his shining gold.

But when Jesus breathed his breath into water and clay,
it became a bird, spread its wings, and flew.

Your praise of God is a breath
from your body of water and clay:
make it a bird of Paradise
by breathing into it your heart's sincerity.

Even Mount Sinai, seeing the light of Moses, began to dance,
became a perfect mystic, and was purified.
Why is it so strange that a mountain should become a wise Sufi—
the body of Moses, too, was of earth.

[*Mathnawi* I: 860–869]

One Task

SOMEONE SAID, "There is something I've forgotten."

There is one thing in the world that you must never forget. You may forget everything else except that one thing, without any cause for worry. However if you remember and take care of everything else but forget that one thing, you will have accomplished nothing. It is as though a king were to send you to a village on a specific mission. You go and perform a hundred other tasks, but if you neglect to take care of the task for which you were sent, it is as though you did absolutely nothing. The human being has come into this world for a particular purpose. If he does not accomplish that purpose, he will have done nothing at all. *We offered the trust to the heavens, and the earth, and the mountains: and they refused to undertake it, and were afraid of it; but the human being undertook it—but, surely, he has been unjust to himself, and foolish* [33:72].

[*Fihi ma Fihi*: Discourse 4]

Free will is the effort to thank God for His gifts:
when you negate free will you ignore that generosity.
Giving thanks for the capacity of will
increases your power;
relying on destiny's course takes the gift from your hand.
Believing in predestination
is like going to sleep on the road—
don't sleep! Don't sleep,
until you come to the gate and reach the threshold!

[*Mathnawi* I: 938–942]

Do the Work While You Can

O master, exert yourself while you can—
follow the way of the prophets and saints!
Making an effort isn't fighting destiny,
because destiny itself has given us this work.
If anyone has ever suffered loss
by following the way of obedience and faith,
I should become an unbeliever.
If your head isn't broken, don't bandage it.
Work to do good while you can,
and then laugh eternally!

[*Mathnawi* I: 975–978]

Keep Digging

Worldly plots are worthless;
but non-attachment to the world
is an inspired strategy.

Let the prisoner plan to dig his way to freedom;
it's foolish to shovel dirt back into the hole.

Though we are prisoners in this world,
we can dig deep and let ourselves out.

[*Mathnawi* I: 980–982]

WE OFFERED *the trust to the heavens, but they could not accept it* [33:72]. Consider how many bewildering feats they perform: they transform rocks into rubies and emeralds; they turn mountains into mines of gold and silver; they cause the plants of the earth to sprout forth into life, making a Garden of Eden. The earth, too, receives seed and produces fruit; it covers faults, and does countless miraculous things beyond description. The mountains produce all kinds of minerals. All these things they do, but that one thing they cannot do—that one task is for the human being to do.

And We have honored the children of Adam [17:70]. Since God did not say, "We have honored the heavens and the earth," it is for the human being to do that which the heavens, the earth, and the mountains cannot do. If he does accomplish this task, his injustice to himself and foolishness are erased. You may object and say that, even though you don't accomplish that task, you do accomplish many other things. But you were not created for those other things. It is as though you were to take a priceless blade of Indian steel, of the sort only found in the treasuries of kings, and use it for cutting up rotten meat and then justify that by saying, "I am not letting this sharp blade stand idle, I'm making good use of it." It is as though you were to use a golden bowl to cook turnips when from one bit of that bowl you could buy a hundred pots. . . . God has set a high price on you, for He says: *See how God has purchased of the faithful their lives and their possessions; in return, theirs is the Garden* [9:111].

[*Fihi ma Fihi*: Discourse 4]

A Knowledge Like Light

What God taught to the bees
doesn't belong to the lion or wild ass.
The bees make a home of juicy sweetness—
God opened the door of that knowing.

What God taught the silkworm—
does any elephant have such expertise?
Adam, though made of earth,
was given knowledge by God,

a knowledge like light
that pierced the Seven Heavens.

[*Mathnawi* I: 1009–1012]

The Dog of Ego

O heart, stay with the pain that is a remedy.
No groaning; endure longing without complaint.
Stamp your foot upon your own desires.
Train the dog of ego. Let this be your sacrifice.

[*Divan-e Shams-e Tabrizi:* Quatrain 311]

External knowledge became a muzzle,
so that one who has faith just in sense-perception
might receive no milk from subtle knowing.

But a jewel fell into the core of the heart
unlike any God gave to the seas or the sky.
How long will you prefer form? O form-worshipper,

has your unreal soul not yet found freedom?
If form defined a human being,
Muhammad and Abu Jahl* would be equal.

The painting on the wall looks like Adam,
but you can see what it's missing—
that magnificent form has no spirit.

Go, seek the jewel that's rarely found!
The Sun of the spirit strikes on the body
from the place where place has no place.

That Sun is not contained in this sky.
This topic is endless.

Knowledge is the seal of the kingdom of Solomon—
the whole world is form, and knowledge is the life-giving spirit.

[*Mathnawi* I: 1015–1030]

---

* Abu Jahl, literally "the father of ignorance," opposed and insulted the Prophet
Muhammad in the earliest days of his mission.

Man has many a secret enemy:
the cautious man is a wise one.
There are hidden creatures, harmful and helpful,
and at every instant their blows strike the heart.
When you go into the river to wash,
a thorn in the water may prick you.
Though the thorn is hidden beneath the water,
you know it is there—you feel it.
The pricks of inspiration and temptation
are from thousands of sources, not just one.
Be patient until your senses are transformed,
so that you may see those hidden ones,
and be delivered from difficulty.
Then you may see whose words you have rejected
and whom you have made your leader.
Taking counsel improves perception and understanding;
the mind is helped by other minds.
The Prophet said, "O you who give counsel,
take counsel with the trustworthy."

[*Mathnawi* I: 1034–1044]

The best of loves has many trials.
A real lover doesn't flee love's tests.
But, when love reaches deep in the soul,
to surrender your life becomes the foreplay.

[*Divan-e Shams-e Tabrizi:* Quatrain 556]

Rind and Robust Seed

Know that these words are like the rind,
and meaning is the seed;
these words are the form,
and meaning is like spirit.
The rind can hide the fault
of the rotten fruit;
it also jealously hides
the secrets of the robust seed.

[*Mathnawi* I: 1097]

Writing on the Water

Whatever you write with the pen of wind
on the parchment of water quickly disappears.
If you expect writing on water to last,
of course you'll be disappointed.

The wind in us is vanity and desire;
when you have abandoned vanity,
it is time for the message from God.
Sweet are the messages of the Maker,
that from first to last won't vanish.

The edicts of kings are transient,
and so are their kingdoms;
all will pass away except
the kingdom and edicts of the prophets,
because the grandeur of kings is from vanity,
while the glory of the prophets is from Divine Majesty.

The names of kings vanish from coins,
but the name of Ahmad* is inscribed forever.
Ahmad is the name of all the prophets:
When the hundredth arrives,
we have the ninety-nine as well.

[*Mathnawi* I: 1099–1106]

---

* Muhammad; literally "the praised one."

YOU SAY YOU ARE BUSY with a hundred "lofty works"; you excuse yourself saying that you are studying jurisprudence, philosophy, logic, astronomy, medicine, and so on. That's all for yourself. You learn jurisprudence so that no one will steal a loaf of bread from you, or take your clothing, or kill you—it's all for your own security. What you learn in astronomy, such as the phases of the heavenly spheres and their influence on the earth, whether it is weighty or light and indicates well-being or danger, is all connected with your own situation. All these serve your self and your own purposes. If the stars appear lucky or unlucky it's still in relation to your own ascendant and your own intentions.

If you consider the matter well, you will realize that the root of the whole business is your self, and all the rest are just branches. Now, if those things that are subordinate to you have so many wondrous subdivisions, consider what you, who are the root, must be like. If your branches have "ascensions" and "descensions," lucky and unlucky aspects, consider what "ascensions" and "descensions" you must have in the world of spirits. Consider what lucky and unlucky signs, benefits and losses you, who are the root, must have that such a spirit possesses such property, is capable of this, and is suitable for such a task.

There is another food for you besides all your sleeping and eating. As the Prophet said, "I spend the night with my Lord, and He feeds me and gives me to drink."*

[*Fihi ma Fihi*: Discourse 4]

---

* This is a hadith (*abitu 'inda rabbi . . .*).

How wide this Ocean of Reason is!
In this sweet ocean our forms are swirling,
floating like bowls on the surface of the sea,
until they become full and sink.

Reason is hidden; only a world of phenomena is seen:
our forms are but the waves or spray of that hidden ocean.
By whatever form we approach the Ocean of Reason,
by that same means the ocean casts forms away.

[*Mathnawi* I: 1109–1113]

Have You Lost Your Horse?

So long as the heart does not see the Giver of its conscience,
so long as the arrow does not see the far-shooting Archer,
one who is that blind thinks his horse is lost.
He's stubbornly spurring his horse along the way,
but he thinks his horse, sweeping him onward like the wind,
    is lost.

That scatterbrain runs from door to door
searching everywhere and asking everyone,
"Who stole my horse; where is he?"
What is that you're sitting on, O master?
"Yes, this is the horse, but where is the horse?"
O you in search of your horse, be aware of yourself!

[*Mathnawi* I: 1114–1119]

God's Light has no opposite at all in existence,
so that by means of it one could make Him manifest:
of course our eyes can't perceive Him, though He perceives all—
witness Moses and Mount Sinai.

Know that form springs from spirit as a lion from the jungle,
or as voice and speech take shape from thought.
This speech and voice emerged from reflection.
You don't know where the sea of that thought is,

but since you've seen the beauty of the waves of speech,
you know that the sea from which they came is gracious.
When waves of thought flew from the Sea of Wisdom,
Wisdom bestowed upon them speech and voice.

The form was born of the Word and died again,
the wave subsided into the Sea.
Form emerged from Formlessness and then returned,
for *truly, unto Him we are returning.**

[*Mathnawi* I: 1134–1141]

---

* This phrase occurs in several places in the Qur'an; for example, *Surah al-Imran*
[3:83]. Everything in existence is in the process of returning to its Source.

THE HUMAN BEING has a guide with him through every endeavor: until an ache awakens within—a yearning and love for something—striving for it will not happen. Without pain one's endeavor will not be fruitful; it doesn't matter whether one is striving for success in this world, the other world, in business, government, academia, the science of the stars, or anything else. Mary did not go to the blessed tree until she experienced the pangs of birth: *and the pains of childbirth came upon her near the trunk of a palm tree* [19:23]. Pain brought her to the tree, and then the withering tree bore fruit. Our body is like Mary, and each of us has a Jesus within, but unless we experience the pains of birthing, our Jesus will not emerge. If there is no pain, our Jesus will return by that hidden way to the original place from which he came, and we will be left deprived.

[*Fihi ma Fihi*: Discourse 5]

O courageous heart, set out on the path of blame.
In every moment strike a blow beyond your own strength.
Every moment kindle a flame in a soul,
and exhale a breath of peaceful ease.

[*Divan-e Shams-e Tabrizi:* Quatrain 1456]

Even though the enemy speaks friendly words to you,
know that his words are a trap,
even though he speaks to you of grain.

If he gives you candy, consider it poison;
if he is kind to your body, consider it cruelty.
When Destiny comes to pass,
you see nothing more than the surfaces of things—
you can't tell enemies from friends.
Since that's how it is, start pleading humbly.
Cry out! Glorify God and start fasting.

Keep crying, "O You who know all that is hidden,
don't crush us beneath the weight of our plotting.
O Creator of the lion, if we have acted like wild dogs,
don't send the lion down upon us from the bush.

Don't make sweet water appear as fire;
don't make fire seem like water.
When You make us drunk with Your wine of wrath,
we see things that really don't exist.

Why are we so drunk that our eyes
are incapable of true seeing,
so that a stone looks like a jewel?"

[*Mathnawi* I: 1192–1200]

He who gave light to my heart
also gave me power.
The light in my heart
strengthened my hand and foot.
He gives us opportunities to rise
and also to bow.
Time and time again,
He shows this help
to those who doubt
as well as to those who can see.

[*Mathnawi* I: 1366–1367]

God spoke into the ear of the rose
and made it laugh in full bloom.
He spoke to the stone and made it a ruby.
He whispered to the body, and filled it with spirit.
He sang to the sun, and it became radiant.
With the slightest caution from Him,
a hundred eclipses cover its face.
Consider what He must have chanted
into the ear of the cloud,
so that it rained profuse tears from its eyes.

And what did He chant into the ear of the earth,
so that it became so silent and circumspect?
Whoever is bewildered and troubled,
God has whispered a riddle into his ear,
so that He might bind him between two thoughts:
"Shall I do what He said or the opposite?"
It is from God that one side weighs more heavily.

To be under the compulsion of Love is to be free.
Other loveless compulsions are like chains.
Love's compulsion isn't compulsion,
it is union with God—
it is the moon emerging from the clouds, shining.

[*Mathnawi* I: 1451–1464]

Joy within Joy

O head, you are cause within cause within cause.
O body, you are wonder within wonder within wonder.
O heart, you are searching within searching within searching.
O soul, you are joy within joy within joy.

[*Divan-e Shams-e Tabrizi:* Quatrain 1668]

A piece of bread wrapped in a cloth remains inanimate,
but digested by a human body
it becomes enlivening spirit.

The human soul transmutes it
with the water of Salsabil.*
Dear reader, such is the power of the soul:
what, then, must be the power of the Soul of that soul?

This bit of flesh which is a human being,
blessed with intelligence and soul,
can split a mountain, divide the sea,
or unearth a mine.

Witness the strength of the soul
in the splitting of rocks and mountains;
the strength of that Soul of the soul
is manifest when *the moon was split apart.*†

If the heart should open the purse of this mystery,
the enraptured soul would rush to the highest of heavens.

[*Mathnawi* I: 1474–1479]

---

* Salsabil is one of the overflowing springs of Paradise.
† *Surah al-Qamar* (The Moon), [54:1].

WITHIN GOD'S PRESENCE there is no place for two I's. You say "I," and He says "I"—either you must die for Him or He for you so that duality might disappear. However, His dying is impossible and inconceivable, because "He is the Ever-Living, the One who does not die." He is so gracious, though, that if it were possible He would die for you so that the duality might vanish. However, since it is not possible for Him to die, you must die, so that He may manifest Himself to you and thereby eliminate the duality.

If you tie two birds together, even though they may be of the same kind and their two wings become four, they will not be able to fly because of duality. If, however, you tie a dead bird to a living one it will fly, since duality no longer exists.

[*Fihi ma Fihi*: Discourse 6]

When the torrent reached the sea, it became the sea;
when the seed reached the corn field, it became the crop of corn.
When the bread reached connection with the human being,
it became living and full of knowledge.
When the wax and firewood were devoted to the fire,
their dark essence became light.
When the dusty stone of antimony entered the eyes,
it turned into sight and became watchful.
Oh, happy is the man who was freed from himself
and united with the existence of one who is living!
Too bad for the living one who kept company with the dead!
He also died; life sped away from him.
When you run for refuge to the Qur'an of God,
you have mingled with the spirit of the prophets.
The Qur'an is the states of the prophets,
those fish of the holy sea of His Majesty.

[*Mathnawi* I: 1531–1538]

By nature, every spirit has the life-giving breath of Jesus,
but one breath wounds, while another heals.
If spirits were freed from the body's veils,
everyone's words could be like the Messiah's.
If you wish to speak words sweet as sugar,
control your body's desires;
don't run after this world.
Children beg for candy;
the intelligent desire self-control.

[*Mathnawi* I: 1598–1601]

WHEN YOU PERCEIVE a fault in your brother, the fault really is within you; you just see it reflected in him. In the same way, the wise are a mirror in which you see your own image. "The faithful are a mirror to the faithful."* Clear yourself of your own fault, because what distresses you in someone else is really within your self.

Any harmful qualities you have in yourself, like injustice, anger, greed, envy, callousness, or pride, don't offend you. Yet when you see them in someone else, you are repulsed and hurt. No one is disgusted by a scab or abscess of his own; anyone will put his own wounded finger in the stew and lick it without feeling squeamish in the least. If, however, you see a tiny abscess or cut on someone else's hand, you would never be able to stomach the stew into which he dips his finger. Harmful moral qualities are just like those scabs and abscesses: no one is troubled by his own, but you suffer distress and become horrified at seeing only a little in someone else.

Just as you avoid someone, you must excuse her for avoiding you when offended by you. Your pain is her excuse, because your pain comes from seeing that which she also sees. "The faithful one is a mirror to the faithful." The Prophet did not say that the denier is a mirror to the denier—not because the denier does not have the possibility of being a mirror, but because he is unaware of the mirror of his own soul.

[*Fihi ma Fihi*: Discourse 6]

---

* This is a hadith (*al-mu'minu mir'ât . . .*). See *FAM* 41, no. 104.

IN THIS WORLD each person is preoccupied with something. Some are preoccupied with love for women, some with acquiring possessions, some with making money, some with acquiring knowledge—and each one believes that his well-being and happiness and ease depend on that. That is also God's mercy. When someone goes seeking after it and does not find it, he turns his back on it. Then after a while he says: "That joy, that mercy must be sought after. Maybe I did not seek well enough. Let me try again." When he seeks again he still does not find it, but he keeps going until the mercy manifests itself without any veil. Only then does he realize that he had been going in the wrong direction.

But God Most High has some servants who see clearly even before the Resurrection. 'Ali, may God be well pleased with him, said, "Even if the veil were lifted my certainty would not increase." By this he meant that if the covering were taken away and the Day of Reckoning were to appear, his certitude would not be greater. It's like when a group of people go into a dark room at night and pray, each facing a different direction—when day breaks they all turn themselves around, all except the one person who had already been facing Mecca all night long. Since the others are now turning to face in his direction, why should he turn somewhere else? Such servants of God face Him even during the night: they have turned away from everything other than Him. For them the Resurrection is immediately present.

[*Fihi ma Fihi*: Discourse 7]

The Touch

The saint gathers pearls
from the depths of the sea;
from what was deeply lost
he brings a treasure to the surface.

And if a perfect saint picks up
a handful of earth, it changes to gold;

but some flawed fellow gathers gold,
and it turns to ashes in the end.
Since a person just and good is welcomed by God,
his hand becomes the hand of God.

[*Mathnawi* I: 1606–1610]

The mouthful that increases our light and perfection
comes from lawful earnings.
If oil arrives and puts out our lamp, it's not oil.
From the lawful morsel are born knowledge and wisdom;
from the lawful morsel unfold tenderness and love.

[*Mathnawi* I: 1642–1644]

Lawful Gambling

I have a love as pure as clear water.
And to gamble for love is lawful for me.
The love others have changes from state to state,
but the love and the Beloved I have are constant.

[*Divan-e Shams-e Tabrizi:* Quatrain 1080]

Without a doubt, action stems from sight:
so the human being is nothing
but the pupil of his or her eye.
I don't dare tell all there is to tell—
those who are at the center keep me circumspect.
Since our forgetfulness and remembrance
are under the Divine wing,
and He comes at our call for help,
every night that Glorious One empties hearts
of hundreds of thousands of good and evil thoughts.
When the sun shines, He fills hearts—
He fills those oyster-shells with pearls.
By God's guidance all former thoughts
recognize the spirits to which they've been attached.
Each morning, your skills return to you,
to open for you the door of livelihood.
The goldsmith's craft doesn't go to the ironsmith;
the smiling of the good-natured man
doesn't go to one who is grumpy.
On the Day of Resurrection
capacities and character will come,
like property you own, to the one who owns them.
Upon awakening, skills and dispositions
come back in haste to the one who claims them as his.
At the hour of dawn, skills and thoughts
return to where they're supposed to be.
Like carrier pigeons, they bring useful knowledge
gained from other places far away
back to their own home.

[*Mathnawi* I: 1679–1690]

ALL DESIRES, affections, loves, and attachments people have for all sorts of things, such as fathers, mothers, the heavens and the earth, gardens, palaces, endeavors, knowledge, food, and drink— one comes to realize that every desire is a desire for the Divine, and these things are all "veils." When one passes beyond this world and sees that Sovereign without these "veils," then one will realize that all those things were "veils" and "coverings" and that all along what everyone was seeking was really that one thing. Every difficulty will then be resolved. All the heart's questions and problems will be resolved, and every thing will be seen face to face. It is not God's way to answer every problem individually, but rather with one answer all problems are solved.

In winter everyone puts on warm clothing and huddles in a warm nook by the stove to escape the cold. Because of that biting cold, all the plants and trees drop their leaves and are without fruit, concealing all that they possess within themselves that they might not suffer from the cold. When spring bursts forth in "answer" by manifesting, all their different "questions" with regards to living, growing things, and dormant things are answered at once; the secondary causes disappear. Everything sticks its head out and knows what caused the upheaval.

[*Fihi ma Fihi*: Discourse 9]

O tongue, you are both the fire
and the hay that's been gathered:
how long will you keep burning this hay?
My soul in secret laments because of you,
even though it does whatever you bid it to do.
"O tongue, you are an endless treasure.
O tongue, you are also an endless disease."*
You whistle to lure birds, and you lend comfort
during the desolation of separation from the Beloved.

[*Mathnawi* I: 1700–1703]

---

* This was a saying of Imam 'Ali, the close companion of the Prophet Muhammad.

JESUS, UPON WHOM BE PEACE, laughed a lot. John the Baptist, upon whom be peace, wept a lot. John said to Jesus, "You have become mighty secure from God's subtle traps to laugh so much."

"You," replied Jesus, "have become mighty heedless of God's subtle and mysterious grace and loving-kindness to weep so much!"

One of God's saints, who was present at this moment, asked God which of the two was of the more exalted station. God answered, "The one who thinks better of me," that is, "Within my servant's conception of me, I am there.* Each of My servants has an image or idea of Me. Whatever each of them imagines Me to be, that I am. I am the servant to images within which God lives; I care nothing for any reality where God does not dwell. O My servants, cleanse your thoughts, for they are My dwelling places.

Now make a trial for yourself and see what is more beneficial to you—weeping, laughter, fasting, prayer, or retreat. Choose whichever of these states serves you best and causes you to advance further."

[*Fihi ma Fihi*: Discourse 11]

---

* This is a *hadith qudsi*, a saying of God conveyed through the Prophet Muhammad outside of the Qur'an (*ana 'ind . . .*).

I can't help thinking of rhymes,
and my Sweetheart says to me,
"Don't think about anything except seeing Me.
Sit comfortably, O My rhyming friend:
in My presence you're rhymed with happiness.

What are words that you should even think of them?
Words are just thorns in the hedges of the vineyard.
I'll swirl word and sound and speech into perplexity,
so that without them I might converse with you.

The word I kept hidden from Adam I'll speak with you,
O you who are the consciousness of all that is.
I'll tell you that word I didn't speak even to Abraham,
and the pain of love even Gabriel does not know."

That word of which Jesus breathed not a word,
and God, from jealousy, did not utter even without *má*.
What is *má* in language? Positive and negative.
I'm not positive, I am selfless and negated.

I have found true being in non-being,
so I wove my selfhood into nothingness.

[*Mathnawi* I: 1728–1735]

All kings are enslaved to their slaves;
everyone is ready to die for one who dies for them.
All kings are in submission
to someone who prostrates before them;
everyone is intoxicated with love
for one who is intoxicated by them.
The hunter becomes a prey to birds
so that at the right moment
he might make them his prey.
The hearts of heart-ravishers are caught
by those who have lost their hearts to them.
All beloveds are the prey of their lovers.
Whomever you consider to be a lover,
regard her, also, as one who is loved,
for she is both this and that.
If those who are thirsty seek water,
know, too, that water is seeking the thirsty.
Since He is your lover, be silent—
He is pulling at your ear, so be all ear.

[*Mathnawi* I: 1736–1740]

SOMEONE ASKED what is better than prayer. As we have already said and explained, the answer is that the "soul" of prayer is better than prayer. Another answer would be that faith is better than prayer, for prayer is obligatory five particular times a day, but faith is continuous. One can be excused from prayer for a valid reason, and it is also possible to postpone a prayer, but faith isn't just dropped or postponed. Faith without prayer is still beneficial, but prayer without faith, like that of hypocrites, has no benefit. Prayer differs from religion to religion, but faith is everywhere the same. Its states, its focus, and so forth are the same.

There are also other differences, and according to the attracting power of the one who is listening, they become apparent. The listener is like flour in the hands of a bread-maker; words are like water sprinkled on the flour according to the need.

[*Fihi ma Fihi*: Discourse 8]

Dissolving Distance

How long will you watch us from a distance?
We offer help and even love is helpless before us.
What is the soul? The tiniest infant in our cradle.
What is the heart? One of our wandering beggars.

[*Divan-e Shams-e Tabrizi:* Quatrain 52]

The Hidden Sweetness

The Beloved said, "O rough-spirited soul,
you haven't valued Me, because you bought Me cheaply."
The one who buys cheaply sells cheaply—
a child will trade a pearl for a crust of bread.

I'm drowned in the kind of love,
in which first and last loves both disappear.
Let me be brief, not explaining everything,
that your senses and this tongue might not burn away.

When I say "lip," it's the "lip" of the Sea I mean;
when I say "nothing," it means "nothing but You."
It's the sweetness that makes my face solemn:
it's the fullness of speech that makes me silent,

so that my solemn face may hide such sweetness,
and conceal it from both worlds, so that this word,
just one of a hundred subtle mysteries
may not enter just any ear.

[*Mathnawi* I: 1755–1762]

Intimacy

For anyone whose prayer-niche
is turned toward revelation,
going back to mere belief is shameful.
For anyone who has become master of the King's robes,
it is loss for him to transact the King's business.
For anyone who is the intimate friend of the Sultan,
it's injury and insult for him to wait at His door.
When the King has granted you
the privilege of kissing His hand,
it's a grave error to kiss His foot instead.
Though you're showing your loyalty
by laying your head at His feet,
in comparison to kissing His hand, it's a mistake.
The King is jealous of anyone
who prefers the distant fragrance
after seeing His Face.

[*Mathnawi* I: 1765–1770]

The drowning man in an agony of soul
clutches at every straw.
Flailing with hand and foot
in the hope someone will take his hand
and save him from danger.
The Divine Friend loves this agitation:
it is better to struggle, even hopelessly, than to lie still.
The Ruler of All is never idle,
though without any agitation;
complaint from Him would be a marvel, for He is not ill.
The Merciful is described as,
*"Every day He is about some new affair."**
In this Way keep working hard:
until your last breath, don't be idle for a moment,
so that your last breath may be a last breath
in which that grace is your intimate friend.
Whatever the soul in man and woman strives to do,
the ear and eye of the soul's King are at the window.

[*Mathnawi* I: 1818–1824]

---

* *Surah ar-Rahman* (The Infinitely Compassionate One), [55:29].

A HUMAN BEING is a wondrous thing: everything is inscribed within him, but "veils" and "cloudiness" prevent him from reading the knowledge within himself. The "veils" and "cloudiness" are various preoccupations, worldly schemes, and desires. Yet, despite all these things that are hidden in the "darkness" behind the "veils," the human being can still read something and is aware of what he reads. Consider how "aware" he will become when the veils are lifted and the darkness disappears and what knowledge of himself he will discover within.

All these different trades—tailoring, building, farming, gold-smithery, astronomy, medicine—innumerable professions—have been discovered from within the human being, not revealed from under rocks and clumps of mud. It is said that a raven taught man to bury the dead*—that came from a reflection of man that fell upon the raven. It was the human being's own urge that caused him to do it, for, after all, animals are a part of the human being.

[*Fihi ma Fihi*: Discourse 11]

---

* It is said that when Cain killed Abel he didn't know what to do with the corpse. Just then he saw two ravens fighting. When one killed the other, he dug a hole to bury the dead raven, and so taught humankind how to bury the dead. See *Surah al-Ma'idah* (The Feast), [5:34].

Those who offer their beauty to auction,
a hundred evil fates will overtake them.
Plots, angers, and envies pour upon their heads,
like water from waterskins.
Jealous enemies tear them to pieces,
and even friends drain their lives away.

Can anyone heedless of sowing in springtime,
know the value of this life?

You must flee to the shelter of God's grace,
that thousandfold downpouring
of grace upon our souls.
What other shelter would you need?
Even water and fire will protect you.
Didn't the sea become a friend to Noah and Moses?

[*Mathnawi* I: 1835–1841]

Caravan upon caravan are journeying
from non-existence toward existence.
Every night all thoughts and understandings
become as nothing, plunged in the deep Sea.
Then at dawn those Divine ones
lift up their heads from the Sea, like fish.

In autumn countless branches and leaves
retreat into the sea of Death—
in the garden the crow clothed in black like a mourner
laments over the withered green.
Then again from the Lord of the land
comes the command to Non-existence,
"Give back what you've devoured!
Give up, O black Death, what you've devoured
of plants and healing herbs and leaves and grass!"

Brother, sister, collect your wits and consider:
moment by moment, continually,
there is autumn and spring within you.
Behold the garden of the heart,
green and moist and fresh,
full of rosebuds and cypress and jasmine;
branches hidden by the multitude of leaves,
vast plain and high palace hidden by countless flowers.
These words, coming from Universal Mind,
are the fragrance of those cypress and hyacinth.

[*Mathnawi* I: 1889–1899]

God has said to the saint,
"I am your tongue and eye;
I am your senses;
I am your good pleasure and your wrath.
Go, for you are one whom God describes as,
'By Me he hears and by Me he sees.'*

You are the Divine consciousness itself.
How could it be right to say,
'You are the possessor of consciousness'?
Since you have become, through bewilderment,
'He that belongs to God,'
I am yours, for, as it is said
'God shall belong to him.'"†

[*Mathnawi* I: 1935–1939]

---

* This refers to a famous *hadith qudsi*: God says, "When my faithful servant draws near to Me through his or her voluntary devotions, then I love him/her and I become the ear with which he hears, the eye with which he sees, the tongue with which he speaks, the hand with which he grasps, the foot with which he walks." Also "*I become his/her ear and eye. . . . He/she sees with the divine Light of God. . . . His heart didn't contradict what he saw,*" Surah an-Najm (The Unfolding), [53:11–12].

† This is also a *hadith qudsi*: He that belongs to God, God shall belong to him (*man kana lillahi kana 'llahu lahu*).

WITHIN A HUMAN being is such a love, a passion and longing, an itch, a desire, that, even if he were to possess a hundred thousand worlds, he would still not find rest or peace. People try their hand at all sorts of trades and professions—they learn astronomy and medicine, and so forth—but they are not at peace because they haven't found what they are seeking. The beloved is called *dil-ârâm** because the heart finds tranquillity through the beloved, so how can it find tranquillity through anything else? All these pleasures and objects of search are like a ladder. Ladder rungs are not places to stay and abide, but rather are to pass through. The sooner one awakens and becomes aware and watchful, the shorter the road becomes and the less one's life is wasted on these "ladder rungs."

[*Fihi ma Fihi*: Discourse 15]

* *Dil-ârâm* means "that which gives the heart tranquility." It is a frequently used term for the beloved.

We are beautiful, so make yourself beautiful.
Be like us, don't be like all the others.
And if you wish to be a mine of jewels
open the deep ocean within your heart.

[*Divan-e Shams-e Tabrizi:* Quatrain 1464]

The Prophet said, "In these days
the breathings of God prevail:
keep ear and mind attentive
to these spiritual influences;
catch these breathings."
The Divine breathing came,
beheld you, and departed:
it gave life to whom it would, and left.
Another breathing has arrived.
Pay attention, friend,
don't miss this one, too.

[*Mathnawi* I: 1951–1953]

Our True Dimensions

Last night inspiration came unexpectedly.
But a morsel of food barred the way.

Some desires you have
become like a thorn in your foot.
You could be a rose garden, but your spirit is wounded.

This thorn-eating existence is like a camel,
and mounted upon this camel is one born of Muhammad.
O camel, on your back is a bale of roses,
from whose perfume
a hundred rosaries grew within you,

yet your inclination is toward thorn-bushes and sand:
I wonder what roses you will gather
from worthless thorns.

O you who in this search have roamed
from one place to another,
how long will you say,
"Where, where is this rose garden?"

Until you extract this thorn in your own foot,
your eye is dark: how will you find your way?
A human being, who cannot be contained in the world,
becomes trapped in the point of a thorn!

[*Mathnawi* I: 1960; 1966–1971]

The Call of Perfection

The rational mind is a denier of Love,
though it may pretend to be an intimate.
It is clever and knowing, but not empty of itself.

Until your angel has become nothing, it is a devil.
In word and deed the rational mind is our friend,
but when you come to the case of intimate feeling,
it's worthless. It's worthless because

it hasn't left its own self-existence;
it didn't willingly become nothing.
Most die unwillingly, but the Spirit is perfection
and its call is perfection.

[*Mathnawi* I: 1982–1986]

"CONSULT YOUR HEART, even if the jurist has given an opinion."*
The truth is within you. Compare it with the jurists' opinion and
when it is in accord, follow that counsel.

When a physician comes to see a sick person he questions
his internal physician—you have a physician within you, that is,
your natural temperament, which accepts what is good for you
and rejects what is bad. So the external physician inquires of the
internal physician about the quality of what you have eaten—
whether it was heavy or light, and how you have been sleeping.
Depending on what the internal physician tells him, the external
physician determines the remedy. So the internal physician, the
temperament, is the main indicator. When he falls ill, and the
temperament becomes corrupt, because of his weakness, he sees
things backward and gives crooked indications—he says sugar is
sour and vinegar sweet. Then he needs the external physician to
help him return to his original balance, so that again he might take
counsel from his own physician.

Now, the human being also has a temperament of the true
self; and when it falls ill, whatever his internal senses see or say is
contrary to the truth. So the saints are physicians who help him
until his natural temperament is restored and his heart and reli-
gion are strengthened. "Show me things as they are!"†

[*Fihi ma Fihi*: Discourse 11]

---

* This is a hadith (*istafti qalbaka . . .*). See FAM 188, no. 597.
† This is a hadith (*arinâ 'l-ashyâ' . . .*). See FAM 45, no. 116.

The Breath of the Saints

The Unseen World has its own clouds and rain,
it has another sun and sky.
Only the elect perceive it;
the rest are *in doubt as to a new creation.**
There is a rain that nurtures;
and there is a rain that brings decay.
The blessing of the spring rain is wondrous,
but the autumn rain is a consuming fever for the garden.
The spring rain nurtures it tenderly,
while the autumn rain renders it sickly and pale.
Know that cold and wind and sun
all produce varied effects—find the clue.
In the Unseen there are also different movements.
Some bring loss and others bring gain;
some a profit, some a swindle.
This breath of the saints is of that spiritual spring
that causes a garden to grow in the heart and soul.
Their breath nurtures like spring's fresh rain.

[*Mathnawi* I: 2035–2043]

---

* *Surah Qaf* [50:15].

The sayings of the saints, whether soft or rough,
are the support of your spiritual life.
Don't defend yourself against them,

Whether the saint speaks hot or cold,
receive his words with joy:
and you will escape from blistering heat
and freezing cold, and from the fires of Hell.

His "hot" and "cold" is life's new season of spring,
the source of sincerity and faith and service.
The garden of souls is living through him,
and the sea of his heart is filled with these pearls.

Yet thousands of griefs lie heavy on a wise man's heart,
if from the garden of his heart even a straw is missing.

[*Mathnawi* I: 2055–2059]

Truly, is there any fair thing
that has not one day lost its luster,
or any roof that did not become a floor,
except the voices of the holy in our breasts,
that resound like the trumpet of resurrection?

By their hearts all hearts are intoxicated.
Through their non-existence we learn to truly be.
The saint is the amber that attracts our thought,
the delight of revelation, the inspired mystery.

[*Mathnawi* I: 2078–2081]

I Am

Don't flee from Me, for I am your buyer.
Look into Me, for I am the light of your eyes.
Enter My work, for I am what will shine in your efforts.
Do not tire of Me, for I am your marketplace.

[*Divan-e Shams-e Tabrizi:* Quatrain 1268]

The Sun of Reality

In the forest of spirit be like a falcon—
venture your life in the hunt,
give your self away like the sun.
The heavenly sun forever diffusing life
is replenished moment by moment.
The Sun of Reality refreshes this old world!
Soul and spirit penetrate humanity
from the Unseen like a gushing spring.

[*Mathnawi* I: 2219–2222]

Intellect is a guide; Love is a friend.
Mind is a river you travel; Love is the water of life.
Although there's no trace of the lover's journey in the heavens,
no one reaches there without the signs of journeying.

[*Divan-e Shams-e Tabrizi:* Quatrain 1098]

SOMEONE IMAGINES that he can rid himself of his negative qualities by means of his own labor and striving. When he struggles and makes every effort possible only to be disappointed, God says to him, "You thought it would come about through your own power and action and effort. This is the law I have established, that is, that whatever you have you should expend it in My Way— only then does My grace arrive.

"We say to you, 'Travel this infinite road with your own weak legs.' We know that with your weak legs you will never be able to accomplish the journey—in a hundred thousand years you would not complete even one stage of the journey. But when you make the effort and collapse and fall down, unable to take another step, then God's loving grace will carry you. Just as a child, while it is nursing, is carried, but when it grows older it is left to walk on its own, even so now when your strength has left you, God's grace carries you. . . .

"Now that you no longer have the means to continue, behold Our grace and favor and loving-kindnesses, how they swarm down upon you. Even after a hundred thousand strivings you would not have seen so much as a tiny bit of this. So *celebrate the praise of your Sustainer, and ask His forgiveness* [110:3]. Seek forgiveness for your thoughts and conceit—you thought that all this could come to you from your own striving. You didn't recognize that it all comes from Us. Now that you have seen that it comes from Us, seek forgiveness." *For He is inclined to forgive* [110:3].

[*Fihi ma Fihi*: Discourse 17]

The sensible man doesn't pay attention
to what increases or decreases,
since both pass like a quickly moving stream.
Whether the water of life runs clear
or is tumultuous as a flood,
don't bother speaking of it—
it doesn't endure more than a moment.

In this world thousands of animals live happily,
without the throes of anxiety.
The dove on the tree coos gratefulness,
even though her food for the night has not yet arrived.

The nightingale's glorification is this:
"I depend for my daily bread,
on You who love to respond."
The falcon delights in the King's hand,
and no longer looks at carrion.

Look at every animal from the gnat to the elephant:
they all are God's family
and dependent on Him for their food.
What a nourisher is God!
All these griefs within our hearts
arise from the smoke and dust
of our existence and vain desires.

[*Mathnawi* I: 2289–2296]

A Piece of Death

Every pain is a piece of death.
Expel that portion of death from yourself,
before the whole of it is poured on your head.
If that portion of death has become sweet,
the whole of death will be sweet.
Every pain is a messenger not to be ignored.
But whoever tries to live sweetly dies painfully:
whoever serves his body doesn't nourish his soul.

[*Mathnawi* I: 2298–2302]

You can spend a hundred days studying,
but the soul won't enjoy your groaning.
You may laugh at me and my story,
but you, O scholar, have not become Majnun*!

[*Divan-e Shams-e Tabrizi:* Quatrain 1729]

---

* Majnun, whose name means "possessed by madness," is the legendary lover of Layla. He was totally immersed in Love.

IF ICE AND SNOW should say, "I have seen the summer sun," or, "The sun of summer has shone upon me," and still remained ice and snow, no intelligent person would believe it. It is impossible for the sun of summer to come out and not melt ice and snow.

Although God Most High has promised recompense for good and evil at Resurrection, still every moment examples of it can be seen. If a happiness comes to a person's heart, it is recompense for having made someone else happy. If he becomes sorrowful, it is because he has made someone else sad. These are gifts from the other world and indications of the Day of Reckoning, so that people may understand the much from the little, just as a handful of wheat is offered as a sample of the storehouse full.

[*Fihi ma Fihi*: Discourse 15]

I'm drunk from a cup engraved with the word "Love."
The horse I ride has Love for its reins.
This Love is a supreme work, and
I am bound to the One who loves his slave.

[*Divan-e Shams-e Tabrizi:* Quatrain 256]

If I catch a snake, I remove its fangs
to save it from having its head crushed.
Its fangs are an enemy to its life,
so with this skill I turn an enemy into a friend.
Never from desire do I chant my spell,
for greed has long ago been vanquished.
God forbid! I desire nothing from created beings:
Through contentment there is
a world within my heart.

[*Mathnawi* I: 2359–2362]

Try being poor for a day or two,
and find in poverty double riches.
Be patient and abandon your distaste for being poor.
For in poverty is the light of glory.
Don't be sour, and you will see
thousands of contented souls in an ocean of honey,
and thousands of bitter souls steeped in rose syrup.
If you had the comprehension,
this tale of my heart
would shine upon your soul.

[*Mathnawi* I: 2373–2376]

These words are like milk from the soul's breast—
but without someone to drink, the flow decreases.
When the listener is thirsty, the speaker,
even though almost dead, is moved to speak.
When the hearer is fresh and yearning,
even the dumb and mute discover their eloquence.

Everything that is made beautiful and fair and lovely
is made so for the eye of one who sees.
How should the sound of melody and treble and bass
be made for the ear of one who is deaf?

Not in vain did God make musk fragrant:
He made it so for the one who can smell,
not for one whose nostrils are blocked by disease.

[*Mathnawi* I: 2378–2382; 2385]

THE HUMAN SOUL is a meeting place of doubt and difficulty, and there is no way for it to be rid of doubt and difficulty except by being in love. Then the doubts and difficulties disappear. "Your love for a thing makes you blind and deaf."*

When Iblis refused to bow down to Adam, in disobedience to the command of God, he said, *"You created me of fire, and created him of clay"* [7:12]. In other words, my essence is of fire and his is of clay. How is it right for one who is superior to bow down to an inferior? When Iblis was cursed and banished for this sin and opposition and contention with God, he said: "Alas, O Lord! You have made everything. This was your temptation of me, and now you are cursing and banishing me!"

When Adam sinned, God Most High expelled him from Paradise and then said: "O Adam, when I took you to task and chastised you for your sin, why didn't you argue with me? After all, you had a line of defense. You could have said, 'Everything proceeds from You. It is You who have made everything. Whatever You will in this world comes to be, and whatever You will not can never come to pass.' You had such a clear, and rightful case. Why didn't you argue it?"

Adam answered, "O Lord, I knew that well, but I could not be impolite in Your presence. My love for You would not allow me to argue with You."

[*Fihi ma Fihi*: Discourse 23]

---

* This is a hadith (*hubbuka li'l-shay'* . . .). See *FAM* 25.

Your intellect is like a camel-driver, and you are the camel:
it drives you in every direction under its bitter control.
The saints are the intellect of intellect,
and in relation to them,
all intellects until the end are like camels.
Come, look carefully upon them with reflection:
there is one guide, and a hundred thousand souls behind him.
What is the guide and what the camel-driver?
Get yourself an eye that might behold the Sun!
See how the world has been left nailed shut in night,
while day awaits, expectantly, relying on the sun.
Here is a sun hidden in a particle,
a fierce lion within the fleece of a lamb.
Here is an Ocean hidden beneath straw—
beware, don't step so quickly on this straw.
A feeling of hesitancy and humility of heart
is a mercy from God,
when it comes to the spiritual guide.
Every prophet came alone into this world—
he was alone,
and yet he had a hundred unseen worlds within him.
Though he enfolded himself within a very small frame,
his power enchanted the macrocosm.
The foolish thought him to be lonely and weak,
but how is he weak
who has become the companion of the King?

[*Mathnawi* I: 2497–2507]

For a time, imitating everyone else,
I preferred myself. Unaware,
I only heard my own name.
Because I was in myself,
I did not deserve to know myself.
Not until I left myself, did I see myself.

[*Divan-e Shams-e Tabrizi:* Quatrain 15]

See the Reality

Don't burn a blanket on account of a flea;
don't waste the day with every gnat's headache.
If you stick with forms, you'll be an idol-worshipper;
let go of the form, see through it to the Reality.
If you're making the Pilgrimage,
seek a pilgrim for your companion,
whether he be an Indian, a Turk, or an Arab.
Don't focus on what he looks like,
see his intention and his aim.

[*Mathnawi* I: 2892–2895]

Until Crushed

The fruit is the reality, the blossom its form—
blossoms are the good news, fruit is the joy that comes.
When the blossom falls, you can see the fruit—
when the one diminishes, the other increases.

How should bread give strength until it is broken?
How should uncrushed grapes yield wine?
Unless the sweet cherry is crushed,
how will it become the medicine?

[*Mathnawi* I: 2930–2933]

Don't Travel Alone

For sure, old wine grows stronger,
and old gold is more highly prized.
Choose a wise elder, for without him
this journey is full of difficulty and danger.

Without a guide you become confused
even on a road you've traveled many times.
Don't travel alone on a Way you've never seen;
don't turn your head away from the Guide.

[*Mathnawi* I: 2942–2945]

"THERE IS NO MONASTICISM in Islam. Coming together is a mercy."* The Prophet always labored for cohesion, since the binding together of spirits has great and weighty effects that do not unfold when people are alone and isolated.

Mosques are built so that the people of a quarter may gather in order that the mercy and benefit might increase. Houses are separate one from another for dispersion—to hide private relations and faults; that is their purpose. Congregational mosques were created so that all the people of a city might come together; visiting the Ka'ba was made obligatory so that people from many cities and regions of the world might gather together.

[*Fihi ma Fihi*: Discourse 15]

---

* This is a compression of two hadith (*lâ ruhbâniyyata . . .*). See *FAM* 189: "There are no bridles or nose-rings or monkhood in Islam; there is no celibacy . . . in Islam." The second hadith (*al-jamâ'atu rahmatun . . .*) is also shortened: "Cohesion is a mercy, and isolation a torment." See *FAM* 21, no. 76.

In the Garden

Didn't I say, don't sit with sad companions?
Don't sit with anyone but those whose hearts are glad.
Since you are in the garden, don't go to thorns.
Sit amidst the roses, jonquils, and jasmine.

[*Divan-e Shams-e Tabrizi:* Quatrain 1518]

Surrender Yourself

Above all devotional acts on the Way
choose the protective shadow of the servant of God.
Each takes refuge in some act of devotion
and so discovers for himself some means of freedom.

Go, take refuge in the shadow of the wise;
escape from the enemy that opposes you in secret.
Of all acts of devotion this is the best—
by this you will surpass every one
who may have outdistanced the rest.

But pay attention: when that wise one
has accepted you, surrender your self—
go, like Moses, under the command of Khidr.

[*Mathnawi* I:2965–2969]

A certain man came and knocked at a friend's door.
His friend asked him, "Who is there?"
He answered, "It's me."
The friend said, "Go away, it's not the time.
There is no place for the raw at this table."
What will cook the raw one
except for the fire of absence and separation?
What will deliver him from hypocrisy?

The wretched man went away,
and for a year he traveled—in separation
from his friend he burned with sparks of fire.
That burned one was slowly cooked,
until he returned and again paced back and forth
before the house of his friend.

With mindful shyness he knocked at the door,
so no word of disrespect might escape from his lips.
"Who is at the door?" his friend called,
"It is thou, O charmer of hearts," he answered.
"Now," said the friend, "since thou art I, come in, O myself.
There was never room in this house for two I's."

[*Mathnawi* I: 3056–3063]

AS THE QUR'AN SAYS, *Am I not your Lord? They answered, Yes, We bear witness* [7:172]. The food and sustenance of the spirits in pre-eternity was the Word of God without letters or sound. Some who were brought out in infancy remember nothing of their former state, and when they hear the Word do not recognize it. These, having totally sunk into infidelity and error, are "veiled." Others remember a little, and yearning for the "other side" arises in them—these are the "faithful." For others, when they hear the Word, their former state, becomes manifest before their eyes, just as it was in the past. Their "veils" are completely removed, and they join within that union—these are the saints and prophets.

[*Fihi ma Fihi*: Discourse 15]

Recite the text, *Every day He is engaged in some work.**
Don't think He is idle and inactive.
His least act, every day, is that He dispatches three armies:
one army from the loins of the fathers toward the mothers,
in order that the plant may grow in the womb;
one army from the wombs to the earth,
that the world may be filled with male and female;
one army from the earth to what is beyond death,
that everyone may behold the beauty of good works.
This discourse has no end.

[*Mathnawi* I: 3071–3076]

---

* *Surah ar-Rahman* (The Infinitely Compassionate One), [55:29].

Whether the feet be two or four,
they traverse one road,
like the double shears that make but one cut.

Look at those two fellow-washermen:
one has thrown the cotton garments into the water,
while the other partner is drying them!

Again the former makes the dry clothes wet:
as though he were spitefully working against the other.

Yet these two opposites, who seem to be in conflict,
are of one mind and acting for one purpose.

Every prophet and every saint has a way,
each leads to God: all are one.

[*Mathnawi* I: 3081–3086]

THE "PERSON OF HEART" is the All; when you have seen that person you have seen everything. As it is said, "All game is in the belly of the wild ass." All creatures in the world are parts of him, and he is the whole.

> All, good and bad, are part of the dervish.
> Whoever is not so is not a dervish.*

Now when you have seen such a dervish, you will have seen the whole world. Anyone you see after him will just be a repetition. Dervish words are the whole among words—when you have heard their words, whatever you may hear afterward is just repetitious.

> If you see him, at any stage,
> it's as though you have seen all people and viewed all of
>   space.

As the poet says,

> O true copy of the Divine Book that you are,
> O mirror of Majestic Beauty that you are,
> nothing existing in the world is outside of you.
> Seek within yourself whatever you desire,
> for that also you are!†

[*Fihi ma Fihi*: Discourse 16]

---

* This line is from Rumi's *Divan-e Shams-e Tabrizi, I, ghazal* 425.
† Rumi is quoting a quatrain by Najmuddin Razi from his *Manarat al-sa'irin*.

Lay the whole of your "we" and "I" before Him—
it is really His kingdom, so give it up to Him.
When you become poor in the right Way,
both the Lion and the Lion's prey become yours.

He is holy, and Glory is His attribute,
so He has no need of anything, whether kernel or rind.
Every prize and every gift of grace that exists
is for the sake of His servants.

The King has no desire—
He has made this whole dominion for His creatures.
Happy is the one who knows this!

Of what use is the possession of any realm,
to the Creator of all realms and both worlds?

[*Mathnawi* I: 3138–3143]

To come empty-handed to the door of friends
is like going to the mill without wheat.
God will say to the people at the Gathering,
"Where is your gift for the Day of Resurrection?
*You have come to Us, alone** without provision,
in the same manner as *We created you.*
Pay attention, what have you brought as an offering—
a homecoming gift for the Day when you rise from the dead?
Or had you no hope of returning?
Did the promise of meeting Me today seem vain?"

Do you, O reader, disbelieve in the promise of being His guest?
Then from the kitchen of His bounty you will get only ash.
And if you are not disbelieving, how do you set foot
in the Court of that Friend with such empty hands?
Give up sleep and food a while:
bring a gift for your meeting with Him.
Like those who sleep but a small part of the night;
in the hours of dawn be of those who asked forgiveness of God.†

[*Mathnawi* I: 3171–3179]

---

* *Surah al-An'am* (Cattle), [6:94]. Both this phrase and the following italicized
phrase come from this verse.
† *Surah adh-Dhariyat* (The Dust-Scattering Winds), [51:17–18].

Stir a little like the fetus that you may be given
the senses to behold the Light.
Then you will leave this womb-like world
and go from the earth into a wide expanse.
Know that the saying "*God's earth is wide*"*
refers to that spacious region where the saints are at home.
The heart isn't weighed down in that spaciousness:
there the fresh boughs of the palm tree
don't become dry and brittle.

Right now you bear the burden of your senses:
You grow weary, exhausted, and stumble.
When you sleep, you're carried aloft;
your fatigue falls away, and your burden,
your pain and anguish, are taken from you.
Consider your sleep as just a taste
of that state in which the saints are soaring.

[*Mathnawi* I: 3180–3186]

---

* *Surah az-Zumar* (The Throngs), [39:10].

THE JURISPRUDENTS ARE CLEVER, and a hundred percent competent in their own profession, but between them and the other world a wall has been created to maintain their realm of *licet* and *non licet*. If that wall were not a barrier for them, they would not want to do what they do and there would be no use for their work....

So a tent was pitched for the king, and He inclined some people to occupy themselves with constructing it. One of these says, "If I didn't make rope, how would the tent be held up?" Another says, "If I didn't make stakes, where would they tie the ropes?" Everyone knows that they are all servants of the king who will come into the tent to gaze upon his Beloved. If the weaver gives up weaving and seeks to become a vizier, the whole world will go naked; so he was given joy in his craft and is content in it. That group, then, was created to keep the world in order, and the world was created for the support of the saint. Blessed is he for whose maintenance the world was created. He was not created in order to maintain the world.

God bestows on every person pleasure and happiness in doing the work that is his, so that even if he were to live a hundred thousand years he would still go right on doing his job. Every day his love for that work increases, and subtle skills develop through practicing his craft, and he derives great joy and pleasure from it.

[*Fihi ma Fihi*: Discourse 21]

Joseph said, "Come, where is your gift?"
The guest, ashamed, sobbed aloud.
"How many a gift," said he, "did I seek for you!
No worthy gift came into my sight.
How should I bring a nugget of gold to the mine?
How should I bring a drop of water to the great Sea of Oman?
I would be bringing cumin to Kirman, the source of all cumin,
if I were to bring my heart and soul as a gift to you.
There is no grain that is not in this barn,
except your beauty, which has no equal.

So all I could bring to you is a mirror
like the inner light of a pure breast,
that you might behold your beautiful face within it,
O you who, like the sun, are the candle of heaven.
I have brought you a mirror, O light of my eyes,
so that when you see your face you might think of me."
He drew forth the mirror from under his arm:
the fair one's business is with a mirror.

What is the mirror of Being? Non-being.
Bring non-being as your gift, if you are not a fool.

[*Mathnawi* I: 3187–3201]

The Dervish

Beyond the body, life, and soul is the dervish.
Better than earth and sky is the dervish.
God's purpose was not to create these worlds,
but the purpose of these worlds is the dervish.

[*Divan-e Shams-e Tabrizi:* Quatrain 255]

Heart and Body

WHEN YOU WANT TO GO somewhere, your heart goes first to see that place and finds out what it is like. Then it returns and takes your body there. People are all "bodies" in relation to the saints and prophets, who are the heart of this world. First, they have journeyed out of their human attributes of flesh and skin; they travel to the other world. They observe both the other world and this world, the depths and heights, and traverse all the stages to understand how to make that journey. Then they return and invite the people, saying, "Come to that original world. This world is a ruin, a perishing abode. We have found a delightful place and have come to tell you about it."

[*Fihi ma Fihi*: Discourse 44]

True Gold and False Coin

When the soul shall turn its coat inside out,
how many followers of the Religion
will be shocked and say, "O my God!"

On the shop counter every gilded coin
that looks like gold is smiling,
because the touchstone is out of sight.

O Coverer of Our Faults, do not lift up the veil from us.
be a protector to us in our final test.
At night the false coin jostles with the gold:

the gold is waiting for day.
With the tongue of its inward state the real gold says,
"Wait, O tinselled one, till the clear day rises."

[*Mathnawi* I: 3293–3295]

The purest mirror is, beyond doubt,
the heart, which can receive an infinity of images.
Moses holds in his breast the formless infinite,
the form of the Unseen that shines
from the mirror of his heart.
Although that form can't be contained in the heavens,
nor in the sphere of the stars,
nor in the earth held up by the Fish,
because all those are limited and numbered,
yet it is contained within the heart—
know that the mirror of the heart has no limit.

[*Mathnawi* I: 3485–3488]

Can a Mirror Ever Lie?

Could a mirror not reflect, or balance-scale lie,
for fear of hurting or shaming anyone?
Mirror and balance are both like touchstones:
even if you beg for two hundred years,
saying, "Conceal the truth for my sake,
display the abundance, not the lack,"
they'll say to you, "Don't be ridiculous:
how can a mirror or balance deceive?
Since we are a means for knowing the truth,
if we fail to display it, what good are we?
If not for us, who else will mirror the face of the fair?"

[*Mathnawi* I: 3546–3551]

IT'S STRANGE FOR YOU to have a state in which there is no room for Muhammad when Muhammad does not have a state in which there is no room for a foul creature like you! After all, the state you have attained is due to his blessing and influence. All gifts are first showered down upon him; then they flow through him to others. That's the way it is. God Most High said, "O Prophet, peace be with you, and mercy and blessings. We shower all gifts upon you." The Prophet responded, *"And* upon God's righteous servants."

God's way was extremely terrifying and blocked by snow. Since the Prophet risked his life first, driving his horse forward in order to clear the way, whoever goes on this way does so through his guidance and grace. He first discovered the way, and left signposts everywhere to say, "Do not go in this direction!" and, "Don't go in that direction!" and, "If you go in that direction, you will perish like the people of 'Ad and Thamud," and, "If you go this way, like the faithful you will find security."

The whole Qur'an expresses this, for *therein are manifest signs* [3:97]. That is to say: We have given signs along these routes. If anyone attempts to tear down any of these signposts, everyone will set upon him, saying: "Why are you ruining our route—do you want to get us killed? Are you a highwayman?" Now realize that the guide is Muhammad. Until one reaches Muhammad, one does not reach us.

[*Fihi ma Fihi*: Discourse 64]

Learn, Turn, and Burn

The heart is your student
for love is the only way we learn.
Night has no choice but to grab the feet of daylight.
It's as if I see Your Face everywhere I turn.
It's as if Love's radiant oil
never stops searching
for a lamp in which to burn.

[*Divan-e Shams-e Tabrizi:* Quatrain 353]

"Give bread, and throw away greed
if you are of my community," said the Caliph Omar.
The people answered, "We've opened our doors;
we've been abundantly devoted to giving."
He said, "You've only given bread
out of obligation and habit,
you haven't extended your hands for God's sake,
but just for the show of it
and your pride and your fame,
not out of awe and humility and prayer."

Wealth is seed—don't plant it in just any salty ground:
don't put a sword in the hand of a thief.
Discern the friends of the Way
from the enemies of Truth—
seek the one who sits with God, and sit with him.
Everyone grants favors to his own folk;
a fool grants favors to the foolish
and thinks he's really done good work.

[*Mathnawi* I: 3714–3720]

A Sanctuary inside a Furnace

If you dwell with the unaware, you become cold,
but if you dwell with the aware, you become a human.
Make a sanctuary inside a furnace, as true gold does,
knowing that if you leave, you will freeze.

[*Divan-e Shams-e Tabrizi:* Quatrain 1705]

Don't let a heart stray
that has been guided with Your grace.
Turn away whatever harm
the Pen of Destiny may have written.

May the suffering in whatever You ordain
not touch our souls.
Keep us connected with those
who are happy with You.

There is nothing more bitter than separation.
Without Your refuge there is only confusion.
Our possessions ambush our real wealth;
our desires tear the garment of spirit from our souls.

Since the harm we do
devours the good we try to reach,
how can anyone save his soul
except with Your protection?

And even if we could protect our own souls,
we still cling to a storehouse of fears,
because the soul is forever distraught with itself,
if it's not in union with the Beloved.

[*Mathnawi* I: 3900–3906]

IN THE FIELDS BENEATH the earth there is a little animal that lives in complete darkness. It has neither eyes nor ears because where it makes its home it doesn't need eyes and ears. Since it has no need for eyes, why should it be given them? It is not because God has a scarcity of eyes and ears, or because He is stingy, but because He gives in proportion to the need. What is not needed becomes a burden.

God's wisdom and grace and bounty remove burdens—why would He impose a burden on anyone? For instance, if you were to give a tailor the tools of a carpenter, an adze, a saw, and a file and tell him to take them, they would become burdens for him since he cannot use them in his work. So God gives things according to need.

Just like the worm that lives in darkness under the earth, there are people who are happy and content in the darkness of this world and have no need for the other world or any yearning to see it. What use would they make of the "eye of insight" or the "ear of understanding"? Their work in this world continues with the sensible eye they have. Since they have no wish for reaching the other side, why should they be given the power of insight, which they would not use?

[*Fihi ma Fihi*: Discourse 25]

The One who grew the garden
has the right to burn it,
because when He tears apart, He can also mend.
Every autumn He shrivels the garden;
but then He makes the rose bloom
that brightens the garden anew,
saying, "O you who were withered,
open, be fresh, become beautiful again!"

The eye of the narcissus grew dark—He restored it;
the throat of the reed was cut—He gave it life.
Since we are the created, not the one who creates,
we must be humble and content.
Everything but Spirit is futile—
truly, that Grace is an abundant cloud
that keeps showering upon us.

[*Mathnawi* I: 3913–3917; 3923]

If all the Divine Wisdom hidden in any particular act
were made known to His servant,
the servant, absorbed by all the benefits of that act,
would be left without the power to perform it;
and the infinite Wisdom of God
will destroy his understanding,
so that he will not be able to do it.

So the Most Exalted offers a small portion
of that infinite Wisdom like a toggle in his nose
and draws him toward that act;
because if He were not to inform him at all
about the benefits, he would never move.
The motive of human actions arises
from perceived advantages to ourselves or others—
that's why we act the way we do.

If He should pour down upon someone
the whole wisdom of his act,
he wouldn't be able to move—
like a camel who will not go forward
unless there is a toggle in his nose,
but also if the toggle is too big
he'll just lie down and refuse.

And there is nothing but We have the storehouses thereof,
*and We only send it down in a certain measure.**

[*Mathnawi* II: Prologue]

---

* *Surah al-Hijr* [15:21].

IT MUST BE REALIZED that everyone, everywhere, is inseparable from his own need. Every living creature is inseparable from its need—each is constantly accompanied by his or her need. It is closer to you than your mother and father; it constantly cleaves to you. Each is bound by that need, tugged this way and that, as though by a bridle. It would be absurd for anyone to bridle himself because a human being is seeking freedom, and it is absurd for one who seeks freedom to be seeking bondage. So, there must have been someone else who has bridled him. For instance, if someone seeks good health, he doesn't try to make himself sick, because it would be absurd to seek ill health while you are seeking good health.

Since you are inseparable from your need, you are also inseparable from the giver of that need. When someone is bridled, he is of course also attached to the bridler pulling him. But because he is paying attention to the bridle, he is weak and powerless. If his gaze were focused on the bridler, he would escape from the bridle. The one pulling the bridle would then be his bridle. He was bridled in the first place because he would not move toward the bridler without it.

[*Fihi ma Fihi*: Discourse 33]

Today

Today the friend of Love cried out in the streets.
If you are him, don't be anywhere but with Him.
Yesterday doesn't exist, don't dwell on that nothing;
and tomorrow hasn't come, don't try to shape it now.

[*Divan-e Shams-e Tabrizi:* Quatrain 998]

Love is uncalculated affection.
That's why it is said that in reality it is the attribute of God
and unreal in relation to His servant.
*God loves them** is the entire sum.
Which of them is really the subject of the words *they love Him?*

And there is nothing but We have the storehouses thereof
and We do not send it down but in certain measure.†

Without water, earth cannot become a brick,
neither will it become a brick when there is too much water.
And the heaven, He raised it and set up the scales.‡
He gives everything according to those scales,
not without calculated balance,
except for those who have been transmuted
from this creaturely state of existence and have become
like those of *And He bestows on whom He pleases*
beyond any reckoning,§
although whoever has not tasted does not know.
Someone asked, "What is love?" I answered,
"You will know when you become 'we.'"

[*Mathnawi* II: Prologue]

---

* *Surah al-Ma'ida* (The Feast), [5:54]. He loves them (*yuhibbuhum*); they love
Him (*yuhibbúnahú*).

† *Surah al-Hijr* [15:21].

‡ *Surah ar-Rahman* (The Infinitely Compassionate One), [55:7].

§ *Surah 'Imran* [3:37]. This is a reference to Mary, mother of Jesus.

When the crows pitch their tents in winter,
the nightingales hide and are mute.
The nightingale is silent without the rose garden,
and without the sun wakefulnesss departs.

O sun, though you disappear from earth's rose garden,
in order to illumine another side of this world,
the Sun of Divine Knowledge has no motion—
its place of rising is within the spirit and the mind.

A perfect Sun shines in the realm of Reality,
illuminating both day and night.
Come to the Sun's rising place:
after that, wherever you go, you'll have that radiance.
After that, wherever you go will be the place of sunrise.

[*Mathnawi* II: 40–46]

O you who study the world, you're just a hired worker.
And you who want Paradise, you're far from the Truth.
And you who are happy with the two worlds, but unaware,
because you have not experienced the happiness of His sorrow,
you're simply excused.

[*Divan-e Shams-e Tabrizi:* Quatrain 1784]

THE FAME OF a certain lion had spread throughout the world. There was a man who was so amazed by hearing of this lion that he set out from afar toward that jungle in order to see that lion. For a year he journeyed, enduring hardships and traveling many stages along the way, until he reached the jungle. When at a distance he saw the lion, he stopped, and could not move closer.

"You have come so far for love of this lion," they said to him, "and this lion has a special quality—he does not harm anyone who approaches him bravely and lovingly caresses him. Only if someone is afraid of him does the lion grow angry. He attacts those who appear to be holding evil opinions about him. You've traveled a whole year and come so close to the lion, why have you stopped now? Take one more step!"

He didn't have the courage to take that one step forward. He said, "All those other steps I took were easy. This one step I cannot take."

What 'Umar meant by faith was that one step forward into the lion's presence. That one step is very great and very rare—it is the concern only of the elect and intimate few. This is what a real step is; the rest are just footprints. Such faith comes only to prophets, those who have washed their hands of their own lives.

[*Fihi ma Fihi*: Discourse 26]

In this world everything attracts something:
the hot draws the hot and the cold the cold.
The worthless sort attract the worthless;
those of enduring worth rejoice among the worthy.
Those of the Fire attract those of the Fire,
those of the Light seek those of the Light.

When you shut your eyes, you felt uncomfortable:
how could the light of the eye
do without the light of the window?
Your discomfort was caused
by the light in your eyes straining
to be joined speedily with the daylight.

If you feel distress within yourself
while your eyes are unclosed,
know that you have shut the eye of your heart.
So open it. Recognize the craving of the eye of your heart,
seeking the immeasurable Light.

                                        [*Mathnawi* II: 81–87]

The Image in the Mirror

SHAIKH SARRAZI was sitting with his disciples, one of whom suddenly had an intense craving for roasted lamb's head. Right away, the shaikh asked for some roasted lamb's head to be brought for him.

"Shaikh," they inquired, "how did you know he wanted that?"

"Because," he replied, "for thirty years I've felt no 'cravings.' I have purified myself and transcended such desiring. I've become as clear as a mirror with no image upon it. When I suddenly had a desire for roasted lamb's head, and when it became intense, I knew that it must be from that fellow. A mirror has no image: if an image appears in a mirror it must come from somewhere else."

[*Fihi ma Fihi*: Discourse 10]

If you're playing chess with a crow,
you'd better not be half asleep. He has good moves,
which will stick in your throat like straw
and be caught there for years.

What is that straw? Desire for status and wealth.
These straws will stick in your throat,
and you'll lose your capacity
to drink the Water of Life.

[*Mathnawi* II: 130–133]

WOE TO THOSE who pray and are heedless of their prayer, who make a show, and deny necessities to the needy [107:4–7]. These words are it: you have the light, but you have no humanity. Seek humanity, for that is the real purpose. The rest is just a lot of talk. When talking goes on and on, the purpose is easily forgotten.

A greengrocer was in love with a lady and sent a message to her through her maid, saying, "I am like this, and I am like that. I am in love; I am on fire; I have no peace; I am tormented. Yesterday I was like this; last night such and such happened to me." And he went on at great length telling his story.

When the maid came to her mistress she said, "The greengrocer sends his greetings and says that he wants to do this and that with you."

"So brusquely?" asked the lady.

The maid answered, "Well, he talked a lot, but that was the gist of it."

It's the gist that matters; the rest just gives you a headache.

[*Fihi ma Fihi*: Discourse 19]

Any life lived apart from spiritual companions
is lifelessness and sleep for your essence.
"Water" that makes you murky is poison,
but "poison" that makes you clear is pure water.

[*Divan-e Shams-e Tabrizi:* Quatrain 750]

It May Not Be What It Seems

If an artful enemy carries off your wealth,
a robber will have run off with a robber.
A petty thief stole a snake from a snake-catcher
and foolishly thought it a prize.

The snake-catcher escaped the snake's bite,
but the man who robbed him
was miserably killed by the snake.

The snake-catcher came upon a dead man,
then recognized him and said,
"My snake stole his life.
My soul had prayed to God
that I might find him and get back my snake.

Thank God my prayer wasn't answered.
What seemed a loss has turned out to be a gain."
Many prayers that would lead to loss and ruin,
the Holy One, from kindness, ignores.

[*Mathnawi* II: 134–140]

IF YOU SPEAK well of another, the good will return to you. The good and praise you speak of another you speak in reality of yourself. An analogy would be the planting of flowers and herbs around your house. Every time you look out you see that garden.

If you accustom yourself to speaking well of others, you are always in the "garden of paradise." When you do good for someone else you become a friend to him, and whenever he thinks of you he will think of you as a friend—and thinking of a friend is as restful and refreshing as a flower garden. When you speak negatively of someone else, you become repulsive in his sight, so that whenever he thinks of you he will imagine a poisonous snake or a scorpion, or sharp thorns and thistles. Now, if you could look at flowers in a garden day and night, why would you wander among thorns and snakes?

Love everyone so that you may always dwell among the flowers in the garden. If you hate everybody, imagining enemies everywhere, it is as though day and night you wander about among thorns and poisonous snakes. That is why the saints love everyone and always think well of people.

[*Fihi ma Fihi*: Discourse 55]

Do Not Bear Malice

Do not bear malice:
if malice leads you astray
your grave will be dug next to the malicious.

Malice is born of Hell,
and your malice is part of it;
it's the enemy of your faith.

Since you can also be a portion of Hell, take care!
The part gravitates toward its whole.
Whoever is bitter will gather with the bitter.

Vain breathings and lies can't be joined with truth.
O brother, you are what you think.
As for the rest of you, it's only flesh and bone.

If your thought is a rose, you are a rose garden;
and if your thoughts are thorns,
you are just kindling for the bath-stove.

[*Mathnawi* II: 273–278]

Go and be kind for Time is aware of kindness,
and He will not take kindness away from the kind.
Material things outlast everyone and will outlast you, too,
but better for you is that kindness will outlast you.

[*Divan-e Shams-e Tabrizi:* Quatrain 644]

I Was a Treasure

It is from My kindness that the smell of fresh bread
awakens hunger in My servant
and causes that living one to weep.

A mother tickles the nose of her babe,
that it may wake and seek its food,
for it may have fallen asleep hungry, unawares,

and on waking it prods her breast for milk.
I was a treasure, a hidden mercy,
so I sent forth a rightly guided, merciful Prophet.*

Every grace that your soul so passionately seeks,
I revealed it to you that you might desire it.

[*Mathnawi* II: 362–366]

---

* This is a *hadith qudsi.*

THERE ARE CERTAIN servants of God who approach God through the Qur'an. There are others, the more elect, who come from God only to find the Qur'an here, and realize that God has sent it. *Surely, We have sent it down; and We will certainly preserve it* [15:9]. The commentators say this refers to the Qur'an. This is fine, but it can also mean: "We have placed in you a substance, a desire to seek, a yearning; We take care of it. We will not let it be wasted; We will bring it to fruition."

[*Fihi ma Fihi*: Discourse 26]

Many Faces

This is what I am: sometimes hidden, sometimes seen.
Sometimes of the faithful, a Jew or Christian,
able to fit into any heart,
taking on a new face every day.

[*Divan-e Shams-e Tabrizi:* Quatrain 1325]

Both the denier and the seeker say "God,"
but there is a big difference between the two.

The beggar says "God" for the sake of bread;
the lover says "God" from his soul.

If that beggar could distinguish the Reality
from the mere name,
neither less nor more would remain before his eye.

Someone talks about "God" for years;
he carries the Qur'an around like a donkey to get his hay.

Had the word on his lips shone forth in his heart,
his body would have shivered and disappeared.

[*Mathnawi* II: 407–501]

On a moonlit night what does the moon
in the mansion of stars
care for dogs and their barking?

The dog is doing his job;
the moon is smoothly fulfilling her task
by means of her bright countenance.

Does the dog's barking
ever reach the moon's ear,
especially that Moon divinely appointed?

The king drinks wine on the bank of the stream till dawn,
and enthralled in the music
is unaware of the croaking of frogs.

[*Mathnawi* II: 416–417; 421–422]

If you are running away in hope of some relief,
in that direction, too, a calamity comes to meet you.
No corner is without wild beasts;
there is no rest but in the place where you are alone with God.

By God, if you flee into a mouse-hole,
you will be afflicted by someone who has the claws of a cat.

People thrive on fantasy if their fantasies are beautiful,
but if their fancies show anything unlovely
they melt away like wax in front of a fire.

If amid snakes and scorpions
God keeps you with the imaginings
of those who are spiritually fair,
the snakes and scorpions will be friendly to you,
because that imagination is the elixir
that transmutes your copper into gold.

Patience is sweetened by this kind of imagination,
since in this case the imaginings of relief come to mind.

Such relief enters the heart from faithfulness:
weakness of faith is despair and torment.
Patience is crowned with faith—
where one has no patience, one has no faith.
The Prophet said, "God hasn't given faith to anyone
in whose nature there is no patience."

[*Mathnawi* II: 590–591, 593–601]

WHEREVER YOU ARE, in whatever circumstances you find yourself, always strive to be a lover, a passionate lover. When love becomes your possession, you will always be a lover—in the grave, at the Resurrection, in Paradise, forever. When you plant wheat, it will surely be wheat that grows; wheat will be in the storehouse, and wheat will be in the oven.

Majnun wanted to write a letter to Layla, so he took a pen and wrote these verses:

> Your name is upon my lips,
> your image is in my eye;
> the memory of you is in my heart—
> where then should I write?

Majnun broke the pen and tore up the paper. Many a person whose heart is full of such words is unable to express them in speech, even though he is a lover in quest and longing. That isn't surprising, and it is no hindrance to love, because on the contrary, what matters in love is the heart, and passion, and yearning. An infant loves milk and is nourished and strengthened by it, yet it cannot describe or define or explain what milk is. No matter how much his soul yearns for that milk, the infant is unable to express in words the pleasure it finds in drinking milk or how it suffers if it is deprived of it. A grown man, on the other hand, may be able to explain and describe milk in a thousand different ways, even though he finds no pleasure or delight in it.

[*Fihi ma Fihi*: Discourse 44]

Reality is what grabs hold of you
and pulls you away from mere things.

Reality is not what makes you blind and deaf
and causes you to cling more tightly.

The spiritually blind imagine things
that only increase their suffering;
the fancies of selflessness
are what come to the eyes of visionaries.

[*Mathnawi* II: 720–722]

Saddle or the Horse?

The blind are a mine of the letters of the Qur'an.
They see the saddle but not the horse.

If you can really see, catch the horse that has bolted.
How long will you merely mend the saddle?

If you catch the horse, you'll have the saddle, too.
Anyone with the spirit of life will not be starved for bread.

The back of the horse can carry your wealth and goods,
but the pearl of your heart
can support a hundred people.

Get up on the horse barebacked.
Isn't that the way of Muhammad?

[*Mathnawi* II: 723–728]

God commanded in a revelation, "O Prophet,
stay in the company of lovers.*
Though the whole world is warmed by your fire,
even fire is smothered by ashes."

[*Divan-e Shams-e Tabrizi:* Quatrain 898]

---

* *Stay patiently by the side of those who call their Sustainer morning and evening, seeking His Face. Surah al-Kahf* (The Cave), [18:28].

GOD OCCUPIED MOSES with the affairs of the people. Even though he was at God's command and was totally preoccupied with God, God occupied one side of him with the people's welfare. Khidr, on the other hand, He kept totally preoccupied with Himself.*

At first, the Prophet Muhammad was kept totally preoccupied with Himself, but later He commanded him to call the people, counsel them, and rectify their condition. The Prophet wept and lamented, "O Lord, what sin have I committed? Why do You drive me from Your presence? I have no desire to be involved with people." Then God said, "Muhammad, do not grieve, for I will not let you become totally occupied with people. Even in the midst of that involvement you will be with Me. Being with Me as you are now will not be lessened one bit while you are occupied with them. In whatever endeavor you are engaged, you will be in complete union with Me."

[*Fihi ma Fihi*: Discourse 15]

---

* Rumi is referring to the story of Moses and the mysterious "servant of God," the immortal Khidr. See *Surah al-Kahf* (The Cave), [18:60–82].

Tether Your Donkey!

The donkey of your ego has run off again!
You could have tethered it.

How long will it run away
from the work and the load, how long?

Let it bear the burden
of patience and thanksgiving,

whether for a hundred years
or for thirty or twenty, at least.

[*Mathnawi* II: 729–730]

The Real Enemy

If you have subdued your egoism,
you no longer have to make excuses:
nobody in the world remains your enemy.

If anyone doubts my words about the prophets and saints,
and should ask, "Didn't the prophets subdue their egoism—
so, why did they have enviers and enemies?"

Listen, O seeker of truth, let's solve this difficulty and doubt.
Those who were deniers were really enemies to themselves:
they were striking at themselves the blows that they struck.

An enemy is one who strikes at another's life;
someone destroying his own life is not an enemy to others.

[*Mathnawi* II: 785–789]

The Light of God has gradations,
seven hundred veils of light.
Behind each veil a certain class of saints
has its place of abode:
these veils of theirs ascend,
rank by rank, up to the finest leader.

Those in the lowest rank,
through the weakness of their eyes,
can't endure the brighter light;
and those at the highest ranks
blink at the light
that is still more advanced.

The Light that is the vibrant life of the highest rank
is heartache and tribulation to the one who squints;
but his squinting, little by little, subsides,
until he passes beyond the seven hundred veils,
and becomes the Ocean of Light.

[*Mathnawi* II: 821–826]

IT IS SAID that in the time of the Prophet, the Companions who knew a chapter or half a chapter of the Qur'an by heart were considered extraordinary and were greatly admired. It was because they "devoured" the Qur'an.

Now anyone who can devour a pound or two of bread may be called extraordinary, but a person who just puts bread in his mouth and then without chewing or swallowing spits it out could "devour" thousands of tons like that. It is about someone like that it is said, "There is many a reader of the Qur'an who is cursed by the Qur'an"—that is, someone who is not aware of the real meaning.

[*Fihi ma Fihi*: Discourse 18]

Erased

Unless the seeker is absolutely erased,
in truth, he will not come into union.
Union is not penetrable. It is your destruction.
Otherwise any worthless person would become the Truth.

[*Divan-e Shams-e Tabrizi:* Quatrain 800]

The dervish bears hardship
the way iron bears the hammer and the fire;
he glows red and happy.
Chamberlain of the fire,
he has an immediate audience with it.

Water needs a pot to boil—
having a container allows
this conversation between water and fire;
without it relationship is not possible.
But the dervish needs no go-between:
the flames touch his very being.

He is the heart of the world,
because by means of this heart
the body attains to its true art.

If the heart is not there,
how can the body speak?
If the heart doesn't seek,
how can the body seek and search?
The dervish that glows with the fire
is the theater of the holy rays;
and so the heart, not the body, is the theater of God.

All lesser hearts are like a body to the heart
of the human being whose heart is complete,
aligned with its original source.

[*Mathnawi* II: 830–834]

Our Original Food

Every soul prefers a different food;
but if that food is not its real food
it needs a change.

Though the clay-eater desires clay,
it's not a sign of health,
nor is it his natural food.

He has lost his natural sense
and his appetite misleads him.
Having given up honey to eat poison,
he imagines the food of disease
to be his nourishment.

Our original food is the Light of God.
Living on material food alone is not for us,
but some disease has caused
our minds to fall into this delusion
that day and night we should eat only that food.

We become spiritually pale, weak, and faint:
where is the food of *heaven's starry tracks*?*
That is the food of the chosen,
food eaten without fork or throat.

[*Mathnawi* II: 1078–1086]

---

* *Surah adh-Dhariyat* [51:7].

I KNOW WELL the rule for God's provision of our daily bread. It is not in my character to run here and there in vain or to suffer needlessly. Truly, if I give up all thought of money, food, clothing, and the fire of lust, whatever my daily portion is will come to me. If I run around in search of my daily portion, the effort exhausts and distresses me. If I am patient and stay quietly in my own place, it will come to me without pain and anguish. For my daily portion is also seeking me and pulling me. When it can't draw me, it comes—just as when I can't draw it, I go after it.

The upshot of these words is this: You should be so engaged in the affairs of the world to come that this world will run after you. What is meant by "sitting" here is sitting in occupation with the affairs of the other world. If a man runs, when he runs for the Way he is truly seated. When he is sitting, if he is sitting for the sake of this world he is running. The Prophet said, "Whoever makes all his cares a single care, God will see to all of his cares."

[*Fihi ma Fihi*: Discourse 49]

Every single bad habit of yours is a thorn bush:
many times you've stepped on these thorns.
Many times you've been wounded by your own bad habits—
common sense would tell you so, but you are senseless.

If you're indifferent to the wounding of others,
which comes to pass from the darkness of your nature,
at least you're not unaware of your own wounds:
you are the torment of yourself and of every stranger.

Either take up your ax and strike
like 'Ali to break through the barrier before you,
or join these thorns with a rose:
bring your fire to God's Light

so that your fire will disappear in His Light,
and all your thorns become roses.

[*Mathnawi* II: 1240–1246]

Wake Up!

The worm is in the root of the body's tree;
these unhealthy roots must be dug out and burned.
Travelers, it is late.
Life's sun is going to set.
During these brief days, while you have strength,
be quick and spare no effort of your wings.

Value the small amount of seed that remains,
in order that eternal life may grow from these few moments.
While this jeweled lamp still glows,
now is the time to trim its wick and replenish its oil.
Wake up! Do not say "Tomorrow"—
for many tomorrows have come and gone.

[*Mathnawi* II: 1264–1269]

Until you've found the pain, you won't reach the remedy.
Until you've given your life, you won't get that all souls are One.
Until you're an Abraham, you won't know the Fire within,
You won't reach the springhead of Life as Khidr* did.

[*Divan-e Shams-e Tabrizi:* Quatrain 1815]

---

* An immortal being who appears as a guide to those in need; the "green man."

A certain king said to a shaikh,
"If you would like some of the riches I have, just ask."

"Your Royal Highness," he answered,
"Aren't you ashamed to say that to me?
I have two ugly slaves, and you are under their power."

"Who are they?" said the King, "There must be some mistake!"

The shaikh replied, "One is anger and the other is lust."

A true king is unconcerned with kingship;
he is someone whose light, without moon or sun,
shines forth from itself.

Only one whose essence is a treasure
can offer gifts from the treasury.

[*Mathnawi* II: 1465–1470]

No matter what plans you make,
no matter what you acquire,
the thief will enter where you least expect.
Be occupied, then, with what you really value
and let the thief take something less.
When a trader's bales fall into the water,
he'll try to grab the most valuable things.
Some things will certainly be lost
as the water of life flows away.
Let go of the cheap stuff
and work to save what's really important.

[*Mathnawi* II: 1505–1509]

Caring for the Bride of Intrinsic Meaning

WHEN YOUR "brides of intrinsic meaning" are manifested within you and the mysteries are revealed, be careful! Again I say, be careful that you do not tell them to others. Do not talk about them, and do not mention the words you hear from us to just anybody. "Do not give wisdom to those unworthy of it, so that you might not wrong it, but don't withhold it from those worthy to receive it, so that you might not wrong them."

If you had a fair beloved hidden in your house and she had said to you, "Do not show me to anyone, for I am yours alone," would it ever be appropriate to parade her around the marketplace, calling to everyone, "Come and see this beauty"? Would your beloved like it? She would be furious with you and run off to someone else. God has forbidden these words to those "others."

[*Fihi ma Fihi*: Discourse 15]

Become a Rose

In Love, if you are comfortable for the space of a breath,
what right do you have to stand with the lovers?
You cannot approach the Beloved with your mind sharp as a thorn;
become a rose and the Beloved will fall into your arms.

[*Divan-e Shams-e Tabrizi:* Quatrain 673]

The vision of God looks into the heart
to see whether there is some modesty there,
no matter what your words sound like,
because the heart is what matters.

Speech is secondary. The essence is what's real.
So what is secondary matters less.
How long must I keep telling this story?

I want burning, burning:
become intimate with that burning!
Light up a bonfire of love in your soul;
burn up thought and speech!

O Moses, those who know the "right" way are of one kind,
but they whose souls and spirits burn
are of another sort.

[*Mathnawi* II: 1760–1764]

Lovers are continually ablaze:
you can't tax a ruined village.

If the lover speaks clumsily,
don't call it a mistake;

and if he's covered in blood,
still he doesn't need purifying.

For martyrs, blood is better than water:
his "fault" is better than a hundred "correct" actions.

Don't ask the love-drunk for specific directions.
What use does a diver have for snowshoes?

Why do you order those whose robes
are rent in pieces to mend them?

When you're within the Ka'ba,
there is no prescribed direction of prayer.

The religion of Love stands apart from all religions:
for lovers, the only religion and creed
is the One Who Cannot Be Described.

[*Mathnawi* II: 1765–1770]

WHEN UTHMAN BECAME caliph he went up into the pulpit. The people waited to see what he would say, but he remained silent and said nothing. He looked steadily at the people, causing such a state of ecstasy to overwhelm them that neither could they leave nor did they even know where they were. A hundred preachings and sermons could never have put them into such a state. Precious lessons were understood by them, and more mysteries were revealed to them than could ever have been communicated through any amount of effort or preaching. Until the end of the assembly Uthman kept looking at them in silence. Just as he was about to descend, he said, "It is better for you to have an active leader than one who speaks." What he said was true—if the purpose of speaking is to communicate something of benefit and to transform character, it was imparted much better without speech than might have been achieved by words. So, what he said was perfectly correct. . . .

The Prophet said, "My Companions are like stars: whichever of them you follow, you will be rightly guided." When you look at a star and are guided by it, it does not speak any words. Yet merely by looking at the stars one knows the right way from the wrong way and can reach one's destination. In the same way, it is possible for you to look at God's saints and for them to exercise influence over you without them saying a word. Without words or questioning your destination will be reached, and you will be transported to your goal, union.

[*Fihi ma Fihi*: Discourse 31]

While your nature is purified through fasting
you'll follow the footsteps of the purified through the universe.
With the burning of the fast, you will radiate like a candle,
but with the darkness of mouthfuls,
you'll just be a morsel for the earth.

[*Divan-e Shams-e Tabrizi:* Quatrain 1929]

This lower mind is just like a donkey:
it can't stop thinking of how to get its fodder.
But Jesus' donkey acquired a soul:
it made a home in intelligence.
In Jesus reason was strong;
his donkey was made lean by a strong rider,
but from the weakness of reason,
this worn-out ass becomes a dragon.

But if you have a guide like Jesus
and he has made you heartsick,
don't forget that your health, too, is from him.
Do not run away from him.
How do you deal with affliction,
you who have the healing breath of Jesus inside?
For in this world there's always a snake
guarding the treasure.

[*Mathnawi* II: 1857–1862]

Humble Yourself

Many have a talent that urges them
to seek fame for themselves,
but in truth it only leads them to disaster.

If you want to save your own head,
humble yourself like a foot,
and put yourself under the protection
of someone rooted in spiritual discernment.

Even if you are a king,
don't put yourself above him.
Even if you are honey,
gather up his rough sugar.

Your own ideas are merely shells,
his are the soul of thought.
Your coins are false,
his are the purest gold.

You are really he, but seek yourself in him.
Coo like a dove, flying toward him.
And if you cannot bring yourself to serve,
know you're in the dragon's jaws.

[*Mathnawi* II: 1983–1998]

You Are Nearer Than Ourselves

Save us from what our own hands might do;
lift the veil, but do not tear it.
Save us from the ego; its knife has reached our bones.
Who but You will break these chains?
Let us turn from ourselves to You
Who are nearer to us than ourselves.
Even this prayer is Your gift to us.
How else has a rose garden grown from these ashes?

[*Mathnawi* II: 2443–2449]

THIS WAY OF POVERTY is a way in which you attain all your hopes. Whatever you may have longed for will certainly come to you on this way, whether it be the conquest of armies, victory over enemies, capturing property and subjugating people, or superiority over one's peers, or eloquence in speaking and writing, or anything else. When you have chosen the way of poverty, all these things will come to you. Unlike other ways, no one who took this way has ever complained. Out of a hundred thousand who took contrary ways and struggled along, maybe one did reach his goal. And even that one was not completely satisfied, because every way has its own twists and turns along the path to the goal, and the goal can only be attained by means of those twists and turns. That way is long, full of pitfalls and obstacles that arise because of those twists, which may end up blocking one's arrival.

However, when you enter the world of poverty and practice it, God bestows kingdoms and worlds upon you that you could never have imagined. You become embarrassed by what you had longed for before. "Oh," you cry, "how could I have sought such a mean thing when such a wondrous thing existed?"

Here, however, God Most High says, "Although now you no longer desire such a thing, and are now disdainful of it, yet it did once cross your mind. Yet you turned away from it for Our sake. Our generosity is infinite, so of course, I will make that, also, easily attainable for you."

[*Fihi ma Fihi*: Discourse 39]

While I am dwelling with you somewhere on earth,
I am coursing above the seventh sphere, like Saturn.
It's not I that is sitting beside you, but a shadow
cast from a bird that flies above thought:

because I have passed beyond thoughts,
and have become a swift traveler farther on.
I am the ruler of thought, not ruled by it,
because the builder is ruler over the building.

All creatures who are ruled by thought
are aching in heart and mired in sorrow.
I yield myself to thought purposely,
but when I will I spring up from among them.

I am a soaring hawk;
thought is just a gnat:
how should a gnat have power over me?
I come down from those high currents,
for the sake of those who need me.

But when disgust at the coarseness of this lowly world seizes me,
I soar up like *the birds who spread their wings,**
not with feathers that have been glued on,
but with these wings that have grown from my essence.

[*Mathnawi* II: 3555–3564]

---

* *Surah al-Mulk* (Sovereignty), [67:19].

BEFORE ATTAINING his goal and becoming famous, the Prophet witnessed the eloquence of the Arabs and wished to be as eloquent and elegant of speech as they were. When the world of the unseen was revealed to him, he became intoxicated in God and lost all interest in that longing. God said to him, "I give to you that very eloquence and elegance of speech you were desiring."

"O Lord," he replied, "of what use is that to me? I don't care about that. I don't want it."

"Do not grieve," said God, "for both the eloquence and your indifference to it shall stand, and it will not be a problem for you." And God indeed gave him such speech that the whole world, from his own time until this present day, have written many volumes of commentary to explain it. They still continue to do so, but still fall short of comprehending it.

Then God said, "Your companions, out of weakness and fear for their lives and fear of the envious, whisper your name. I will publish your greatness abroad, and it will be cried out aloud five times a day in graceful tones from lofty minarets throughout the regions of the world, from east to west."

Anyone who gambles himself upon this way will find all his goals, worldly and religious, made easy. Of this way no one ever complains.

[*Fihi ma Fihi*: Discourse 39]

WE REALIZE THAT faith is discernment. After all, the basis of jurisprudence is Divine revelation, but as it got mixed up with the ideas, emotions, and the application of people, that grace vanished. So, now what resemblance does it bear to the subtlety of revelation?

Consider the water that flows from a spring in Turut into the city. See how clear and pure it is at its source. When it enters the city and passes through the gardens, quarters, and houses of the inhabitants, so many people wash their hands and feet and faces and other parts in it, and their clothes and carpets, and the urine and filth of all the quarters and of horses and camels are poured into it and mix with it. Then see what it is like when it emerges on the other side of town. Even though it is the same water—it will turn dirt into mud; it will slake the thirst of the thirsty; and it will turn the pasture green—still it takes a discerning person to comprehend that the water has not kept its purity and that unpleasant things are now mixed into it.

"The faithful one is discerning, wise, understanding, and intelligent," [as the Prophet said]. An elder is not intelligent if he is preoccupied with playing; even though he may be a hundred years old, he is still immature and childish. And a child, if he is not preoccupied with playing, is an elder. Here, age doesn't matter.

Incorruptible water [47:15], that is what is needed. "Incorruptible water" is that which cleans all the impurities of the world without being tainted. It remains as pure and clear as it ever was, neither disintegrating in the stomach nor becoming adulterated or polluted. That is the Water of Life.

[*Fihi ma Fihi*: Discourse 39]

The sciences of Wisdom are God's armies,
by which He strengthens the spirits of the initiates,
and purifies their knowledge from the adulteration of ignorance,
their justice from the adulteration of bias,
their generosity from the adulteration of ostentation,
and their forbearance from the adulteration of foolishness;
and brings near to them whatever was far from them
in their understanding of the hereafter;
and makes easy to them whatever was hard for them
in respect of obedience and energetic endeavor.

[*Mathnawi* III: Prologue]

Someone who searches for water in the desert
will not be prevented from seeking it by his knowledge
of what is contained in the seas, and he will be earnest
in seeking the Water of this spiritual Life
before he is cut off from it by preoccupation
with the means of earning a living
and hindered by illness or want,
and before other objects come between him and that goal
to which he is hastening,
since no one who prefers vain desire or is inclined to ease
or turns back from his search or has fears for himself
or feels anxiety about his means of livelihood
will ever attain to Knowledge,

unless he takes refuge with God
and prefers his spiritual affairs to his worldly affairs
and takes from the treasure of Wisdom the great riches,
which neither lose their value
nor can be inherited like worldly riches,
and the majestic lights and noble jewels
and precious mansions of Wisdom,
giving thanks for His abundance,
glorifying His special consideration,
and magnifying His apportionment.

[*Mathnawi* III: Prologue]

Learn, Teach, and Be Gentle

A person will not attain Knowledge
unless he seeks refuge with God
from the crudeness of distractions
and from an ignorance so blind
that he makes much of the little that he sees in himself
and belittles the much and great which is in others,
and admires himself for that self-conceit,
which God would never approve.

But it is good for one who has knowledge
and is seeking
that he should learn whatever he does not know,
and teach others what he knows already,
and deal gently with those of weak intelligence,
and neither be made conceited by the stupidity of the stupid
nor harshly rebuke one who is dull of understanding.
*Such were you were before, but God has been gracious to you.**

[*Mathnawi* III: Prologue]

---

* *Surah an-Nisa'* (Women), [4:94].

A Lamb Knows Its Mother

WHEN BAYAZID WAS a child, his father took him to school to learn jurisprudence. When he was brought before the teacher, Bayazid asked, "Is this the jurisprudence of God?"

"This is the jurisprudence of Abu Hanifa," they answered.

He said, "I want the jurisprudence of God!"

When he was taken before the grammar teacher, he asked, "Is this God's grammar?"

The teacher answered, "This is Sibawayh's grammar."

"I don't want it," he replied. Wherever his father took him, he said the same thing. So, unable to do anything with him, his father left him alone.

Still searching, he later came to Baghdad. As soon as he saw Junayd, he cried out, "This is the jurisprudence of God!" And how should a lamb not know its mother, having been nourished by her milk? Bayazid was born of intelligence and discernment. Let go of the outer forms.

[*Fihi ma Fihi*: Discourse 39]

God is transcendent and exalted
above the insults of darkened minds,
and the superstitions of those ignorant of Oneness,
and the fault-finding of those without knowledge,
and the comparisons of Him by the comparers,
and the evil conceptions of the thinkers,
and the descriptions by those who only vainly imagine . . .

He is the Helper to Success and the Giver of Abundance,
and to Him belongs the power
of conferring abundant benefits and grace,
especially upon His servants, the knowers,
despite some who desire
to extinguish the Lights of God with their mouths—
but God will bring His Light to completion,
despite those in denial.
Truly, We have sent down this Reminder
and truly We will guard it.
And whoever alters it after he has heard it,
surely the guilt of that is upon those who alter it:
truly, God is Hearing and Knowing.
And praise be to God, the Sustainer of all creatures!*

[*Mathnawi* III: Prologue]

---

* *Surah al-Hijr*, [15:19], *Surah al-Baqarah* (The Cow), [2:181], and *Surah al-Fatiha*
(The Opening), [1:2] are combined in this weaving of Qur'anic passages.

Don't Be Mistaken

As long as I have life, I am the slave of the Qur'an.
I am dust at the door of Muhammad the Chosen.
If anyone makes anything else of my words,
I am disgusted with him and whatever he says.

[*Divan-e Shams-e Tabrizi:* Quatrain 1331]

The arc of heaven, which is so stable,
is not held up by ropes or pillars.
The power of Gabriel was not from the kitchen;
it was from beholding the Creator.

The power of the saints of God comes from God,
not from meat or trays of food.
Their bodies, too, have been molded of Light,
so that they have transcended the Spirit and the Angel.

Since you are gifted with the qualities of the Almighty,
pass beyond the fire of the ego's illness,
like Abraham, the intimate friend;
so that the fire might become
for you, also, *cool and a sanctuary.**

[*Mathnawi* III: 5–10]

---

* *Surah al-Anbiya'* (The Prophets), [21:69].

What Else Can I Do?

It's not possible to carry my heart anymore.
It's better that my yearning take it from me.
If I don't give my heart to the longing I have for You,
what else could I do with it? Why would I have it?

[*Divan-e Shams-e Tabrizi:* Quatrain 1089]

The secrets of the Divine Majesty
are drunk by the ear
of one who like the lily
has a hundred tongues
and is speechless.
The grace of God bestows
a throat on the earth,
so that it might drink water
and make a hundred plants grow green.

[*Mathnawi* III: 21–22]

Why You Must Change

From the moon to the fish there is nothing in creation
that doesn't have a throat to draw sustenance from God.

When the spirit's throat is empty of concern for the body
its portion is worthy of a sovereign.

To receive this royal sustenance you must change,
because negative people die due to their negativity.

When a human being gets used to eating dirt,
he pales, becomes sickly and miserable,

but when his foul character has been transformed,
ugliness vanishes from his face, and he radiates like a candle.

[*Mathnawi* III: 41–45]

If you don't perceive
how the leaves applaud,
you need a spiritual ear,
not the ear of the body.

Close the ear of the head
to witty chatter and lying,
that you might behold
the radiant city of the soul.

The ear of Muhammad draws out
the hidden meaning in words,
because as God says of him
in the Qur'an, *"He is an ear."**

[*Mathnawi* III: 100–102]

---

* *Surah at-Tawbah* (Repentance), [9:61].

O Daf, tell the secrets hidden in the diaries of the lovers.
O hand, keep the rhythm with blood-pulsing veins.
O voice of the singer, go deeper and deeper into the heart,
take me from this salty somewhere to that infinite nowhere.

[*Divan-e Shams-e Tabrizi:* Quatrain 1411]

Every Breath You Take

Your life is like a purse of gold:
day and night are like money changers.
Continually Time counts out that gold,
until your purse is emptied and death is here.

If you dig away at a mountain
and don't replace anything of what you've taken,
a desolate land is left behind.

So for every breath you breathe out,
put another in its place.
*Fall in worship and draw near**
so you may reach your aim.

[*Mathnawi* III: 124–127]

_____

* *Surah al-'Alaq* (The Connecting Cell), [96:19].

All night a dervish was crying, "Allah!"
until his lips grew sweet with praise of Him.
The Devil came up to him: "Hey noisy one,
after calling so many 'Allahs,'
where is the response of 'Here I am' to all these 'Allahs'?
I don't hear any response coming from the Throne—
how long will your sad face keep crying 'Allah'?"

The man's heart broke and he fell asleep.
Dreaming, he saw Khidr in radiant green.
Khidr said to him, "You've stopped praising God—
why have you repented of having called Him?"
The dervish said, "Because no 'Here I am'
came to me in answer, I feared
that I might be one who is denied His Door."

Khidr said, "God wants you to know
that every 'Allah' of yours is His 'Here I am,'
and that your prayer and grief and longing
are His message to you. God is telling you:
Your efforts to find a way to Me
were My drawing you to Me,
and it freed your feet from their bonds.

Your trepidation and your love
are the rope to catch My blessing—
beneath every 'O Lord' of yours
is many a 'Here I am' of Mine."

[*Mathnawi* III: 189–197]

Step as a Blind Man Steps

If you have eyes, don't walk blindly;
and if you don't, take a staff in your hand.
If you don't have the staff
of watchfulness and wise judgment,
follow someone who can see.
If you have no staff of discernment,
don't step onto the road without a guide.
Step in the way a blind man steps,
so that your foot might miss the ditch and the dog—
a blind man steps carefully with caution
so that he might not fall into difficulty.

[*Mathnawi* III: 276–280]

The Need for Approval

Shut your eyes so the heart may become your eye,
and with that vision look upon another world.
If you can step away from your need for self-approval,
all that you do, top to bottom, will be approved.

[*Divan-e Shams-e Tabrizi:* Quatrain 808]

The Roots

When a thief carries off a person's property,
his heart starts to tighten.
He says, "I wonder what this contraction is!"
"It's the distress you caused that person."

When the thief pays no attention,
an unrelenting wind fans the flame,
and that contraction gripping his heart
becomes like a policeman in pursuit—
inevitably such thoughts catch up.

The pangs turn into prison and the cross—
the tightening is the root from which branches will sprout.
Any inward contraction or expansion is a root.
When it's a harmful root, quickly cut it down,
so that an ugly thorn might not grow in the garden.

You've felt the contraction—seek a remedy for it,
because every fruit grows from some root.
You've felt the expansion—water that expansiveness,
and when its good fruit appears,
share that with your friends.

[*Mathnawi* III: 355–363]

What You Live By

You who live by the life of this world,
shame on you. Why do you live like this?
If you don't want to be dead, never be without love.
Die in love if you want to be truly alive.

[*Divan-e Shams-e Tabrizi:* Quatrain 1608]

Who is Joseph? Your God-seeking heart,
bound as a captive in your abode.
You've tied your Gabriel up to a post—
hundreds of times you've wounded
his feathers and his wings.
You serve him roast meat;
you take him into the hay barn
and put straw before him,
saying, "Eat! What a choice meal for us,"
but for him the only food
is meeting God face to face.

[*Mathnawi* III: 398–402]

O Reckless One

"Even though you are reckless
and a worshipper of idols,
I will answer when you call Me."
So hold fast to prayer and keep crying out—
in the end it will deliver you
from the hands of every fantasy.

[*Mathnawi* III: 756–757]

The mention of Moses has tied up your thoughts,
you think these are stories that happened a long time ago.

Talking about Moses is a mask—
the Light of Moses is your real concern.

Moses and Pharaoh are both within you:
you need to look for these two adversaries within your self.

The birthing from Moses continues until the Resurrection—
even though each lamp may seem different, the Light is the
        same.

This clay lamp and its wick may appear to be different,
but the Light isn't—it comes from Beyond.

If you keep looking at the glass of the lamp, you'll be lost,
because it's from the glass that multiplicity is seen.

Keep focusing on the Light, so you'll be free of duality
and the multiplicity of colors of this limited body.

[*Mathnawi* III: 1251–1257]

The Way to Bliss

The secrets of Reality are not revealed with questions,
nor by the sacrifice of money and all you own.
Unless eyes and heart bleed for fifty years,
no one finds the way from mere words to bliss.

[*Divan-e Shams-e Tabrizi:* Quatrain 1085]

The whole of the matter is this:
when a man has attained to union,
he doesn't need a go-between.
When you've reached the object of your search
to keep searching for knowledge is harmful.
When you have risen to the roofs of Heaven,
O graceful one, it's useless to look for a ladder.
After having attained felicity,
to focus on the way you came to felicity is pointless
except for the sake of teaching and helping others.
The shining mirror, which has become perfectly clear—
it would be foolish to grind away at it.
Seated happily beside the Sultan, within His graces,
it would be foolish to send a letter by messenger.

[*Mathnawi* III: 1400–1405]

God brought the saints to this earth,
as a mercy to all creatures.
A saint calls people to the Door of Grace,
and he calls to God: "Please, grant them release!"

He keeps trying to warn people,
but when they don't listen,
he cries to God, "Don't shut the door!"
Ordinary people may show mercy now and then;
the saint's mercy is expansive and universal.

His personal mercy has been absorbed in the whole—
the mercy of the Sea becomes the guide.
O you who have just a personal mercy,
come merge with the universal.

Then take Universal Mercy as your guide, and go.
When you are just a part, you don't know the way to the Sea—
you think just any pool is like the Sea.
When someone doesn't know how to get to the Sea,

how could he be a guide;
how could he lead the people there?
When he becomes united with the Sea,
then like a rushing river he shows the way.

[*Mathnawi* III: 1804–1812]

How the Grape Seed Transcended Itself

Through companionship a grape grows from the earth.
But first a grape seed graciously consorted
in solitary intercourse with the dark earth—
it effaced itself entirely in the ground,
until no color or scent, no red or yellow hue remained.

After that effacement, its constriction ceased—
it opened its wings, expanded, and sped on its way.
Since it became selfless in the presence of its origin,
it transcended its limited form
and its real essence was revealed.

[*Mathnawi* III: 2066–2070]

You, ignorant of the marrow, deceived by the skin,
be aware. The Beloved is at the center of your soul.
The essence of the body is sensation
and the essence of the senses is the soul.
When you transcend body, senses, and soul, all is He.

[*Divan-e Shams-e Tabrizi:* Quatrain 322]

"O You who have given, free of cost,
a hundred eyes and ears,
and, without us even asking,
have granted intellect and understanding,
You have bestowed the gift before it was deserved,
despite our complete ingratitude and rudeness:

You are able to pardon
the greatest of our sins in secret.
We have burned ourselves with our desire and greed,
and it is You who give us the blessing of offering a prayer.
We come to You in awe
because You taught us to call
and You lit the lamp of supplication in this darkness."

This is how Daquqi prayed for the people,
like a faithful mother, tears flowing from his eyes,
and that plea rose up to Heaven from him
while he was unconscious of himself.
That unconscious invocation is, in truth, different:
it's not from him—it really comes from God.
God is making that invocation,
since that person has disappeared—
the call and the answer, both are from God.

[*Mathnawi* III: 2212–2224]

Like Foxes We Play with Our Tails

Foxes, in the chase, are saved by their legs,
but these foxes believe their tails saved them!
And so they play fondly with their tails,
thinking, "Without you I'd be dead."

O bold-eyed fox, save your legs from being broken;
without legs, what use is your tail?
We are like foxes, and the noble saints are like our legs:
they save us from a hundred kinds of reprisals.
Our subtle contrivings are like our tails:
we play fondly with our tails, left and right.
We wag our tails in argument and cunning,
in order that so-and-so may be amazed at us.
Our seeking to impress people,
our eagerly grasping at Divinity,
all the guile we use to catch hearts,
has left us in a ditch, unaware.

You are in a ditch, you rascal!
So don't try to twist someone else's mustache!
Unless you yourself have found the Garden,
don't pull anyone's sleeve to try to lead them.
If you're not first a servant of the Beloved,
don't wish to make yourself a sovereign.
In your desire to impress others,
you've tied a noose around the neck of your soul.
O fox, abandon this tail of contrivance,
and devote your heart to the lords of the heart.

[*Mathnawi* III: 2227–2236; 2239–2241]

How could someone who is, himself,
like a straw in the wind of desire,
discern the oppressor from the oppressed?
First deal with the oppressor in yourself,
your own frenzied ego.

A dog always growls at the poor and helpless;
so far as it can, it snaps at the poor.
But know that lions act differently,
because a lion would be ashamed
to prey on neighbors.

[*Mathnawi* III: 2434–2438]

Yourself without Yourself

If you go on the Way, they will open the Way to you.
And if you become nothing, you'll be led to real being.
And if you will be humble, the universe will not contain you,
and you will be shown yourself, without yourself.

[*Divan-e Shams-e Tabrizi:* Quatrain 742]

When a child's lap is filled with shards of pottery,
he trembles for them, as though he owns riches.
If you take a piece away from him, he cries,
and if you give it back, he smiles with laughter.
The child doesn't know that neither his weeping
nor his laughter matter very much.
Because the rich man saw what is just a loan as his own,
he trembled, worried for that false wealth.
That rich one dreams he is wealthy
and fears the thief who might carry off his gold.
When Death pulls at his ear and startles him from slumber,
then he laughs at his fears.

It's the same trembling of these learned scholars
who have such intelligence and knowledge of this world.
Of these accomplished, intelligent men,
God said in the Qur'an, *They do not know.**
Each one is afraid of someone's stealing—
he thinks he possesses great knowledge.
He says, "They're wasting my time,"
but his time is not really of benefit.
He says, "The people take me away from my work,"
but his soul is plunged in idleness up to the throat.
He knows a hundred thousand unimportant things,
but that untruthful one doesn't know his own soul.

[*Mathnawi* III: 2636–2646; 2648]

---

* *Surah ar-Rum* (The Byzantines), [30:6–7].

Pay attention, just look at the loving-kindness of God!
Would anyone but God do this—
be content with a single thank-you for such gifts?
He gives us a head and asks for just one bow of thanks;
He gives us feet and asks for just a moment's pause in prayer.

[*Mathnawi* III: 2672–2673]

If you don't want your friend of today
to be unfriendly tomorrow,
choose friendship with the wise.
You're seasick from the storms of the ego,
because you make everything stormy.
If you take a jewel in hand, it loses its luster;
near you kindness of heart becomes hatred;
and even a beautiful word becomes vulgar.

You say, "I've heard this all before;
tell me something else, my friend."
If something fresh and bright is shared,
the very next day you're cranky and bored.
Get rid of this illness! When it's gone,
every old tale becomes new,
and makes the wayside ditch
burst into blossom.

[*Mathnawi* III: 2691–2699]

Sleeping in Security

IF ANYONE FALLS ASLEEP while we are speaking, his sleep is not from heedlessness but rather from security. It's like when a caravan keeps on traveling through a dark night, over a difficult and frightful road, fearing attack by bandits, and then as soon as people in the caravan hear a dog barking or rooster crowing they know that they have come to a settlement where they can rest. They relax and sleep securely there. On a road where there was no noise or barnyard uproar they were afraid to sleep. In a settlement where they are secure, they can sleep peacefully and happily despite the barking of dogs and crowing of roosters.

Our words also come from a secure settlement; they are the sayings of the prophets and saints. When spirits hear the words of friends they recognize, they feel secure. They are freed of fear, because from these words wafts the fragrance of hope and felicity.

Out of fear, someone traveling in a caravan on a dark night constantly imagines thieves are attacking. He longs to hear the words of his fellow travelers and to recognize them by their voices. When he hears them he feels secure.

"Say, 'Recite, O Muhammad,' for your essence is subtle and cannot be reached with mere sight. When you speak, people comprehend that you are a familiar friend of their spirits, and they feel secure and peaceful."

[*Fihi ma Fihi*: Discourse 44]

We are the spiritual physicians, students of God—
the Red Sea saw us and parted.
Those physicians of the body aren't like us,
they need to check the heartbeat to know a heart.

We see into the heart without any instrument—
we see clearly from a high meadow.
They are physicians of food and fruit:
through them only the bodily self is strengthened.

We are physicians of actions and words,
inspired by a ray of the Light of Majesty—
we know that one deed will be beneficial for you,
while another will block your way,

and some words will bring you blessing,
while others will make your heart ache.
Some physicians need to test your urine;
we take God's inspiration as our test.

We ask no payment from anyone,
because our income flows from a Holy Place.
Come to us, one by one, with that incurable illness!
We are a remedy for the spiritually diseased.

[*Mathnawi* III: 2700–2709]

The Prophet, on whom be peace, said,
"Truly, God Most High has friends who are concealed."

Haven't you seen how the people of this bazaar of ours,
the prophets and the saints, are successful in business,
and what mines of treasure have appeared to them
from entering the shop of non-existence,
and how they have gained in this market?

To one the fire falls into service, like an anklet;
to another the sea lifts him on its shoulders;
to one iron becomes soft and submissive as wax;
to another the wind rises at his command.

And there are others who remain so very hidden:
they possess all this, and yet no one's eye
falls upon their sovereignty even for a moment.
How would the superficial people know them?

They and their miracles are in a holy sanctuary:
even other saints don't hear their names.
Will you remain unaware of the gifts
and the One who is calling you to this?

The world of the six directions is brimming
with this abundance: wherever you look,
you see His bounty.
When such a generous one calls you into this fire,
come in, and don't say, "It may burn me."

[*Mathnawi* III: 3100–3109]

Anas, son of Malik, had a guest
who related that after a meal
Anas saw the table napkin was stained yellow,
and he told his maidservant,
"Throw it into the oven at once."
And that is just what she did.
After a short time she took it out of the oven,
clean and white and without stain.

The guests were amazed
and wanted to know how it didn't burn,
and how it became clean.
Anas, that revered companion of the Prophet,
answered, "Muhammad
often wiped his hands and lips on this napkin."

O heart, afraid of the torment of fire,
be near such a hand and lip as that!
Since it bestowed such honor upon a lifeless cloth,
what will it reveal to the soul of a lover!
Since the Prophet made the stones of the Ka'ba
the *qibla** toward which the faithful turn,
O soul, be humble as earth before the truly holy ones
to win the struggle with your own ego.

[*Mathnawi* III: 3110–3120]

---

* The direction of prayer; the point of orientation.

My Only Answer

Whatever mistakes I may make, You are enough as my balance.
Even if my life is ruined, You are enough as my goal.
I know that when I'm ready to leave this world, they will ask,
"What have you done?" As my answer, "You" will be enough.

[*Divan-e Shams-e Tabrizi:* Quatrain 1812]

Even if sorrow conquers the horizons,
someone held by Love will not be sad.
A single speck of dust that danced with Love
will conquer this world and the next.*

[*Divan-e Shams-e Tabrizi:* Quatrain 410]

---

* "This world and the next" is literally "the two worlds," i.e., the seen and the
Unseen.

What Is Really Going On Here

I am a mountain echoing the voice of the Friend.
I am a picture painted by the Beloved.
I am a just a lock, but you hear His key turning.
Do you think any of these words are mine?

[*Divan-e Shams-e Tabrizi:* Quatrain 207]

GOD'S TREASURIES are many, and God's knowledge is vast. If a person reads *one* Qur'an knowledgeably, why should he reject any *other* Qur'an?

I once said to a Qur'an reader, "The Qur'an says: *Say, If the sea were ink for the words of my Lord, truly the sea would fail, before the words of my Lord would fail* [18:109]. Now with fifty drams of ink one can write the whole Qur'an. So, this is only a symbol of God's knowledge; it's not the whole of his knowledge. If a druggist puts a pinch of medicine into a piece of paper, would you be so foolish as to say that the whole of the drugstore is in the paper? After all, in the time of Moses, Jesus, and others, the Qur'an existed—that is, God's Word existed, it just wasn't in Arabic."

This is what I was trying to make that Qur'an reader understand, but when I saw that it was having no effect I left.

[*Fihi ma Fihi*: Discourse 18]

Conscious Glorification

Conscious choice is the salt of devotion;
otherwise there would be no merit:

this celestial sphere revolves involuntarily,
and so its movement has neither reward nor punishment—

how you use your free will
will count at the time of the Reckoning.

All created beings, indeed, keep glorifying,
but that glorification without will
earns no wages.

[*Mathnawi* III: 3287–3289]

What are these austerities of the dervishes for?
The trials of the body are the everlasting life of the spirit.

Unless a traveler enlivens the everlasting life of her self,
why would she deplete her body?

Why would she move her hand to altruistic work
unless she sees a benefit for her soul?

The only one who gives without any expectation
is God, is God, is God;

or the friend of God who has taken on the nature of God
and become Absolutely Radiant.

[*Mathnawi* III: 3349–3353]

Unless a child sees an apple for the taking,
it won't give up the stinking onion in its hand.

All these salespeople are waiting in their shops
in the hope of making a sale:
they offer a hundred fine articles of merchandise,
and within their hearts they are intent on profit.

O man of the Way, you will not hear a single *salaam*,*
which eventually does not want something from you.

I have never heard a disinterested *salaam* from high or low,
except the *salaam* of God; and I give that *salaam* to you.

Come, seek that *salaam* from house to house,
from place to place, and from street to street!

From the mouth of the man who has a good scent,
I heard both the message and the greeting of God;
and in the hope of that, I am listening with my heart
to the greetings of peace of all the rest
as though they were sweeter than life.

The saint's greeting has become the greeting of God
because he has set fire to the household of self.
He has died to self and become living through the Sustainer—
so God's mysteries are on his lips.

[*Mathnawi* III: 3355–3365]

---

* *Salaam*: the greeting of "peace," wishing blessing for another.

It is Love that makes people happy.
It is Love that fills happiness with joy.
It is Love that birthed me, not my mother.
A hundred blessings and praises to that Mother!

[*Divan-e Shams-e Tabrizi:* Quatrain 449]

You Remain

Your fragrance is always with me.
Your Face never leaves my sight.
Day and night I've been longing for You.
My life is spent, but my desire for You remains.

[*Divan-e Shams-e Tabrizi:* Quatrain 450]

O heart, throw your clothes down upon the way,
and cover your face with the shirt of Joseph.
You're just a small fish; you can't live without water.
Don't think about it, just throw yourself into this stream.

[*Divan-e Shams-e Tabrizi:* Quatrain 936]

I've called that Unlimited Beneficence a garden,
because it's the source of all abundance
and the gathering of all gardens;
and yet, it's "something no eye has seen"*:
how could one ever call it a "garden"?
Yet God called the Light of the Unseen "a lamp."
Parables are offered so that one who is bewildered
might catch the fragrance of that which is Real.

[*Mathnawi* III: 3405–3407]

---

* This is referring to a *hadith qudsi*: The Prophet said, "God says, 'I have readied for My righteous servants what no eye has ever seen, and no ear has ever heard, and no heart of man has ever conceived.'"

A certain friend said to the Prophet,
"I'm always being swindled in commerce.
The deceit of everyone who sells or buys
is like magic and leads me off the track."

The Prophet said, "When you fear
being duped in a commercial transaction,
stipulate that you shall have three days
in which to change your mind,
for deliberation is surely from the Merciful;
while your haste is of the Devil."

When you throw a morsel of bread to a dog,
he first smells it before he eats.
O careful one, he smells with his nose;
we, too, who are endowed with wisdom,
smell that which is given to us
with a purified intelligence.

[*Mathnawi* III: 3494–3499]

A few well-sifted almonds are better
than handfuls of sweet ones mixed with the bitter.
The bitter and the sweet may sound the same when poured,
but the problem lies at their core.

The unfaithful one is weakhearted,
because he relies on opinion;
he has his doubts about the reality of the other world.
He travels along the road, but doesn't know its stages:
one who is blind in heart steps timidly.
When the traveler doesn't know the way,
what can his journey be like?
He journeys hesitatingly, with anxious heart.
If anyone says to him, "Hey! That's not the way,"
he'll stop, frozen with fright.

But if a traveler's wise heart knows the way,
why should he worry?
Don't journey with the fainthearted,
though in boasting they may be
as strong as the magic of Babylon;
in the moment of difficulty
they'll desert you and run away.

[*Mathnawi* III: 4025–4033]

Magic makes a straw a mountain by trickery;
or again, it shrinks a mountain into a straw.
It makes ugly things beautiful by sleight of hand;
and by spreading false words makes beautiful things ugly.

The work of magic breathes spells
and at every breath transforms realities.
In one moment it makes a man look like a donkey,
in another it makes an ass look like a respectable man.

Such a magician is latent within you:
truly, there is a concealed magic in temptation;
but in a world where the magic arts are practiced,
there are magicians who conquer sorcery.

In the plain where this insidious poison grew,
the antidote has also grown.
The antidote says to you, "Seek protection with me,
for I am nearer than the poison to you.

The ego's words are magic and your ruin;
my words are lawful magic and counter that charm."

[*Mathnawi* III: 4070–4078]

Love is from the Infinite, and is eternal.
The seeker of love is not held up by time.
Any heart that is not in love will be useless
on the morning when resurrection removes its veil.

[*Divan-e Shams-e Tabrizi:* Quatrain 754]

God says: "With heavy chains I am dragging you
from the direction of Hell to the everlasting Paradise."

Every blind follower in this Way, be he good or evil,
is being dragged, bound like that, into His Presence.

All go along this Way in chains
of fear and tribulation, except the saints.

People are dragged along this Way reluctantly,
except those who grasp the mysteries.

Work so your inward light might become radiant,
so that your traveling and service might be made easy.

You take children to school by force,
because they are blind to the benefits;

But when a child becomes aware, he runs to school,
and his soul expands with joy.

A child hates to go to school
when he sees nothing of the wages for his work;

when he receives a single coin earned by his skill,
then he works through the night without sleep like a thief.

Make an effort so that the wages for obedience might arrive—
then you will envy the surrendered.

[*Mathnawi* III: 4580–4589]

The command *come against your will*
is for the blind follower of religion.
Come willingly is for the sincere.
The former loves God for something else,
while the sincere one has a pure, real love.
The former loves the Nurse,
but for the sake of the milk,
while the other has given his heart
for the sake of the Nurse Herself.
The child is blind to Her beauty—
he just wants milk,
while the other is truly the lover of the Nurse—
single-mindedly, passionately in love.

[*Mathnawi* III: 4590–4594]

The walls of Paradise aren't lifeless plaster like other walls.
Like the door and wall of the body,
they're endowed with knowing.
The House of Paradise is living
since it belongs to the One Who Gives Life.
Trees, fruit, and clear water converse
with the inhabitant of Paradise,
because Paradise hasn't been built with bricks and wood,
but with good deeds and intentions.
This bodily house is made of inert water and earth,
while that House arises from energized devotion.
An earthly house has a foundation in need of repair,
but the foundation of the House of Paradise,
like the rest of it, is built from knowledge and action.
Throne, palace, crown, and robes are all in conversation
with the one who dwells there.
The carpet there is folded without the carpet spreader;
the House of Paradise is swept without a broom.

Behold the house of the heart, disordered by worldly cares;
yet without a housekeeper it was swept clean
by a vow of repentance.
Its furniture arranged itself without toil;
and the clapper on its door resounds like music.
The life of this everlasting abode exists in the heart—
if it doesn't come to my tongue,
why keep trying to describe it?

[*Mathnawi* IV: 473–482]

A Mirror for the Moon

Dear one, there is a way from your heart to my heart,
and there is an awareness in my heart because of seeking it,
because my heart is like pure sweet water,
and pure water holds the mirror for the moon.

[*Divan-e Shams-e Tabrizi:* Quatrain 334]

If I say that between the tongue's description
and the eye of certainty
there is a journey of a hundred thousand years,
that's small in comparison with the reality.

But, come, don't despair! When God wills,
in a single moment light arrives from heaven.
Every instant His power causes
a hundred influences from the stars
to reach into the darkest mines.

The star of heaven dispels the darkness;
the star of God never wanes in His Attributes.
O you who seek help, the celestial sphere,
though it may be a five hundred years' journey,
is actually close to the earth.

Saturn is a journey of three thousand five hundred years,
but its energy continually acts upon the earth.
But with the return of the sun, God rolls it up like a shadow—
in the sun's presence how can the length of a shadow stand?

And from the pure star-like souls
replenishment keeps coming to the stars of heaven.
The outer aspect of those stars may rule us,
but our inner essence has become the ruler of the sky.

[*Mathnawi* IV: 512–520]

How Are You Being Caught?

O you who are enslaved by this world,
you whose spirit is imprisoned,
how long will you call yourself lord of the world?
Worldly riches are a trap for weak birds;
the kingdom of the next world is a trap for the noble,
so that by means of that kingdom, which is a very deep trap,
the really majestic birds might be caught in God's snare.

[*Mathnawi* IV: 647–648; 652]

There was a stream passing through a deep chasm:
a thirsty man climbed a tree nearby and threw walnuts into it.
One by one, the walnuts were falling into the water;
the sound was reaching his ears, and he could see the bubbles.

A sensible person called to him, "Stop, O youth!
Truly the falling of the walnuts will just increase your need
the more the fruit falls into the water,
because it's a great distance below you.
They will have been carried far away
before you with effort come down from the top of that tree."

He replied, "My purpose in this scattering
is not collecting walnuts.
Look more keenly, don't stop there.
My purpose is that I might hear the sound of the water
and that I might see the bubbles on its surface."

What, indeed, is the thirsty man's business in this world?
To circle forever around the water reservoir,
around the channel, around the Water,
and the sound of the Water,
like a pilgrim circumambulating the Ka'ba of Truth.

[*Mathnawi* IV: 745–752]

O you who surrender to seeking,
good manners are simply forbearance
with anyone who is unmannerly.

When you see someone complaining
of another's ill nature and bad temper,
know that the one complaining
is the one who is bad-tempered,
because he is speaking ill of the other.

Only one who is quietly forbearing
toward the bad-tempered and ill-natured
is really good-tempered and mannerly.

[*Mathnawi* IV: 771–774]

A TEACHER IS INSTRUCTING a child in writing—when he starts to write, the child scribbles a line and shows it to the teacher. In the teacher's view it is all wrong and terribly written, but because of his own skill and consideration, he says: "That's very nice. You've written very well. Very good, very good. Just this one letter here is wrong. It ought to be like this. Oh, and that one, too, you have written incorrectly." Only a few letters out of the whole line does he call bad, and he shows the child how they ought to be written; the rest he praises, so that the child might not lose heart. The child's inability is corrected through such praise, and gradually he is taught and helped on his way.

[*Fihi ma Fihi*: Discourse 31]

We have great affections toward this earth,
because it lies prostrate in humility.
In one moment We bring forth from it a spiritual sovereign;
in another We make it frenzied with love
in the presence of that majesty:
because of him hundreds of thousands of lovers and loved ones
cry out with longing, and increase their seeking.
This is Our work, that renders confused and bewildered
one who has no spiritual inclination.
We confer this eminence on the earth
for the same reason We place a portion of food
before the needy—
because the earth has the external form of dust,
though inwardly it shines with all the qualities of radiance.
Its outside is at war with its inner reality:
inwardly it glows like a jewel,
while outwardly it's like a common stone.
Its exterior says, "We are this, and no more";
inwardly it says, "Look well before and behind!"
Its outside denies it and says the inside is nothing;
its inside says, "We will show you the Truth: wait and see!"
Its outside and inside are struggling:
Divine aid rewards this patient endurance.
We make the forms of existence from this sour-faced earth:
We make manifest its hidden laughter,
for though outwardly the earth is all sorrow and tears,
within it there are hundreds of thousands of laughters.
We are the Revealer of the mystery, and Our work is just this,
that We bring forth hidden things from concealment.

[*Mathnawi* IV: 1002–1014]

The earth has birthed many wondrous children,
but Muhammad has surpassed them all.
Earth and heaven laugh and rejoice,
saying, "From our wedding such a king is born!"
Heaven is bursting with joy because of him;
earth has become a lily through his purity.

[*Mathnawi* IV: 1017–1019]

O fair earth, since your outside and your inside
are at war with each other—
whoever is at war with himself for Spirit's sake,
so that his inner reality might oppose mere color and scent,
if his darkness is in combat with his light,
the sun of his spirit will never set.

The Infinite assures us:
"Whoever struggles for Our sake,
Heaven will put its back under her feet."
Your form is wailing because of the darkness,
while your spirit is like roses within roses.

[*Mathnawi* IV: 1020–1024]

Until a servant becomes erased completely,
*Tawhid** is not realized as real.
Tawhid doesn't descend into you; it is to be naughted.
The unreal doesn't become real by your saying so.

[*Divan-e Shams-e Tabrizi:* Quatrain 800]

---

* *Tawhid* is the oneness of existence, usually affirmed with the phrase: *There is no god but God (La illaha il Allah).*

Three States of Service

THE HUMAN BEING has three spiritual states.

In the first he pays no attention to God but adores and serves and worships anyone and anything—woman, man, wealth, children, stones, land.

Next, when he acquires a certain knowledge and awareness, he serves nothing but God.

Finally, when he progresses in this state, he falls silent: he says neither "I do not serve God" nor "I do serve God"—he has transcended both states. No sound comes from such people into the world.

[*Fihi ma Fihi*: Discourse 53]

A king is seated inwardly amid the rose garden of Union,
while in the outer world he serves as a guide for his friends.
The garden goes with him wherever he goes,
but the people can't see it.

The fruit keeps begging, "Eat me";
the Water of Life is calling, "Drink me."
Without feathers or wings, circle heaven,
like the sun and the full or new moon.

Then you'll move, like spirit, without a foot;
you'll taste of a hundred delicacies without chewing a morsel.

Neither will that monster, Pain, dash against your ship,
nor will ugliness appear in you from aging.

You will be sovereign, army, and throne, all together:
you will be both the fortunate and Fortune, itself.

[*Mathnawi* IV: 1102–1108]

What the Prophets Build

Be greedy in the practice of religion and in good works:
They are still beautiful, even when the eagerness is gone.
Good works are beautiful in and of themselves,
not through the reflection of any other thing;
if the glow of greed departs, the glow of good remains.

But when the glow of greed departs from worldly work,
only black ash remains from what once were red-hot coals.
Foolish capers excite children's greed for fun,
so that with a light heart they canter away on a stick-horse.
But when that excitement ebbs,
the child stops and laughs at the others,
saying, "What was I doing? What did I see in this?"
With greedy excitement vinegar appears to be honey.

The edifice of the prophets was raised without greed;
that's why the splendors of its renown increased without pause.

The grandeur that accrued to the Ka'ba
was derived from Abraham's acts of pure devotion.
The excellence of what the prophets build
is not from earth and stone,
it is from the absence of hostility or self-interest
in the one who is building.

[*Mathnawi* IV: 1130–1139]

In an orchard a certain Sufi laid his face upon his knee
for the sake of mystical contemplation;
then he sank deep down into himself.

An impertinent fellow was annoyed by his semblance of
    slumber.
"Why," said he, "do you sleep?
Look at these vines, these trees, and signs.
Obey the command of God, for He has said, '*Behold*':
turn your face toward these signs of Divine Mercy."

"O man of vanity," he replied, "its signs are within the heart:
that which appears outwardly is only the sign of the signs."
The real orchards and greenness are in the essence of the soul:
the reflection of that upon the exterior world
is like a reflection in a flowing stream.

In the water there is only a reflected image of the orchard—
it shimmers with the passing of the water.
The real orchards and fruit are within the heart.

[*Mathnawi* IV: 1358–1365]

The world is green, with gardens everywhere,
all of it reflected from a beautiful rosy smile,
all around a blazing jewel from a deep mine,
and on every side souls joined with souls.

[*Divan-e Shams-e Tabrizi:* Quatrain 1858]

Many skilled fingers that were once
the envy of master craftsmen
have trembled in the end.

And the soulful intoxicating narcissus-eye—
see how at last it became dull and watery.

The heroic lion who rushes in among the ranks of lions—
finally is vanquished by a mouse.

The acute, farseeing, artful genius—
soon becomes as imbecile as an old ass.

The musk-scented curls that took your reason away—
at last became like the rough white tail of a donkey.

Observe the world's existence,
and how in the beginning it is pleasing and joyous,
and how it is disgraceful and corrupt in the end—

it has displayed its snares and wiles plainly:
it has plucked out the fool's mustache in front of you.
So don't say, "If the world had not deceived me,
I and my reason would have fled from its snare."

[*Mathnawi* IV: 1604–1611]

When did two prophets ever oppose each other?
When did one ever try to wrestle
the other's miracles away from him?
Though the ego may be wise and clever,
its aim is this world, so consider it as dead.

Yet when the Water of God's inspiration reaches that dead one,
the living one arises from the body's tomb.
But until that inspiration comes,
don't be fooled by the rouge of "May your life be long!"
Seek the celebration and remembrance that doesn't die,
the resplendence of the sun that doesn't set.

[*Mathnawi* IV: 1652; 1656–1659]

If riches are consumed in charity,
a hundred lives come to the heart in exchange.
A sowing of pure seeds in God's earth,
and then no income! Impossible.
God's earth is a spacious place;
truly, the produce of God's earth is infinite—
even a single seed multiplies seven-hundred-fold.

You say, "Glory be to God!"
Where are the signs in you of *those who glorify*?
Neither within or without is there a trace.
The gnostic's glorification of God is real,
because his feet and hands have borne witness to it.
It has lifted him up from the obscurity of the body
and redeemed him from the depths of the prison of the world.
On his shoulder he carries the sign of that glory—
the silken robe of devotion
and the Light that goes with him wherever he is.

Their praise of God, like the garden's praise in spring,
has a hundred signs and a hundred splendors.
Fountains and palms and herbs and rose-beds
and plantings of brightly colored flowers
bear witness to their burgeoning spring.

[*Mathnawi* IV: 1758–1771]

How You Must Travel

Though the road is endless, take the first step;
watching from a distance is not for real men.*
To live for the body is all animals can do,
but you must travel by the life of the heart.

[*Divan-e Shams-e Tabrizi:* Quatrain 288]

---

* Forgive the gender-specific translation, but it is truer to the meaning here.
Any man or woman should get the point.

The Itch of the Fool

From one itchy person
a hundred others catch that itch,
especially the itch that is lack of intelligence.
May it not befall even one who is unfaithful.

The unfortunate stars of the fool keep the cloud rainless.
The envious owl makes the whole city a desert.
Because of the itch of the foolish
the Flood of Noah devastated a whole world in disgrace.

The Prophet said, "Whoever is foolish is our enemy
and a demon who waylays the traveler."
Whoever has intelligence is dear to us as our soul.
His breeze is our sweet basil.

If intelligence berates me, I should be pleased,
because it has the emanation of spiritual energy.
Its insult is not without use,
that hospitality is not without a table.

But if the fool puts some sweet to my lip,
I'll catch a fever from tasting it.
If you have any illumination, know this for sure,
that kissing the ass of an ass has no savor.

[*Mathnawi* IV: 1943–1952]

Discernment

From the Face of the Sun you glowed like the moon;
from the company of sulfur you caught fire.
You try to see the unpleasant as pleasant—
he may not change, but you may become unpleasant.

[*Divan-e Shams-e Tabrizi:* Quatrain 1721]

Intelligence is the feast, not bread and roast meat:
the light of intelligence, my son, is the soul's food.
Man has no food but the Light—
the soul doesn't obtain nourishment from anything but that.

Little by little cut yourself off from these material foods—
for they are the food of an ass, not that of a free man—
so that you might become capable
of absorbing that original food
and become accustomed to eating delicate morsels of Light.

It's from the reflection of that Light
that this bread has become bread;
it's from the overflowing of that rational soul
that this animal soul has become soul.

Once you eat of the Light
you won't be attached to the bread and oven.

[*Mathnawi* IV: 1954–1959]

Don't trouble your friend with your egoism,
so that you don't make your friend your enemy.
Do good to people for God's sake
or for the peace of your own soul,
so they may always be friendly in your sight,
and that ugly ideas arising from hatred
may not enter your heart.

[*Mathnawi* IV: 1978–1980]

YOUR MIND IS AT EASE. How is that? Because the mind is a precious thing—it is like a net, and a net must be in good repair to catch prey. When your mind is disturbed, then the net tears and is useless.

So, neither love nor enmity for anyone should go to excess, because either could tear the net. Moderation is needed. Now, "the love that should not be excessive"—I mean by that love for other than God. With regard to the Creator, excess is inconceivable. The greater the love, the better. When your love for someone other than God becomes excessive, you wish him or her constant good fortune, and that is impossible, because all people are subject to the constantly turning wheel of fortune. Since the human condition is constantly in flux, when you wish constant good fortune for someone, your mind becomes disturbed. Similarly, when your enmity for someone becomes excessive, you wish him constant ill fortune and bad luck; yet the wheel of fortune keeps turning and so his conditions change, sometimes favorably, sometimes unfavorably. Since it is not possible for him to be unlucky all the time, your mind again becomes disturbed.

On the other hand, love for the Creator is inherent in the whole world and in all people—Zoroastrians, Jews, Christians— all creatures. How could anyone not love the One who gave him being? Although such love is inherent in everyone, certain barriers keep it veiled. If those barriers are removed, that love will surface.

[*Fihi ma Fihi*: Discourse 56]

The Key Is in Your Hand

Look at humanity, how lacking in light people are,
how they perish out of desire for perishable things.

Because of pride they keep separate from God,
dead to the spirit, living a lie.

Isn't it amazing how their spirits are imprisoned,
while all the while they hold the key in their hands!

[*Mathnawi* IV: 2032–2034]

O you who stab the selfless ones with the sword,
you are stabbing your own body with it. Beware!
For the selfless one has passed into God and is safe:
he is dwelling in safety for ever.

His form has passed away and he has become a mirror:
nothing is there but the image of the face of another.
If you spit at it, you spit at your own face;
and if you strike at the mirror, you strike at yourself.

And if you see an ugly face in that mirror, it's you;
and if you see Jesus and Mary, that is you.
He is neither this nor that: he has simply
placed your own image before you.

When the discourse reached this point, it closed its lips;
when the pen reached this point, it broke in pieces.
Close your lips, O my soul:
though eloquence is at your command, don't breathe a word—

God best knows the right way.
O you who are drunk with the wine of love,
you are near the edge of the roof:
sit down or else descend, and peace be with you!

[*Mathnawi* IV: 2138–2147]

To one who regards only the appearance,
what is the difference between the counterfeit coin and the true?
How should he know what is really in the date basket?
There is much gold that is blackened with smoke,
so that it might be saved from the hands of every envious thief.
There is much copper gilded with gold,
so that the counterfeiter might sell it
to those of little understanding.
We, who see the inward reality of the whole world,
see the heart and are not caught by the outer form of things.

[*Mathnawi* IV: 2172–2174]

Sit with true human beings;
bring the mirror close to the polisher.
What a joy it is to sit next to a true soul,
not like a rock on a pile of rubble.

[*Divan-e Shams-e Tabrizi:* Quatrain 1079]

Keep Polishing

Listen, be watchful if you want a clear heart,
for something is born to you from every action.
And if you have an even greater hope than this,
and if the work goes beyond the rank of one who's watching,
even though you're dark as iron,
practice polishing, polishing, polishing,
so that your heart might become a mirror full of images,
with a lovely lighthearted one shining from every direction.
Though the iron was dark and lacking light,
polishing cleared the darkness from it.

[*Mathnawi* IV: 2467–2471]

WORDS ARE BUT "shadows" of reality. They are like a branch of reality. If the "shadow" can attract, how much more so can the reality!

Words are pretexts; it is sympathy that attracts one person to another, not words. If a man should see a thousand prophetic or saintly miracles, it will be of no benefit to him if he has no sympathetic resonance with the prophet or saint. It is that sympathetic quality that unsettles and agitates. Were there no sympathy to amber within straw, then straw could never be attracted by it. The sympathy between them is veiled; it can't be seen.

What are we talking about? In reality there is only one "attractor," though it appears to be many. Don't you see how a person often has a hundred different desires? "I want noodles. I want pastry. I want sweets. I want fritters. I want fruit. I want dates." These appear to be many different desires that have been expressed by the tongue. The origin of them all, however, is one— hunger. Don't you see that when this same person has had his fill of any one of these things he will say, "I don't need anymore of the rest"? So it's obvious that there were never ten things or a hundred, but just one.

[*Fihi ma Fihi*: Discourse 2]

The Attracting Power of Likeness

Hell flees from the sincere
just as the sincere one flees
with all his soul from Hell,
because his light is not
compatible with the Fire.
The seeker of the Light
is really the opposite of the Fire.

It is related in the sayings of the Prophet
that when the sincere one seeks protection from Hell,
Hell also begs for protection from him,
saying, "God, keep him away from me!"

It is the attracting power of likeness:
what you're attracted to reveals who you are.
Now consider with whom you are congenial.

[*Mathnawi* IV: 2711–2716]

ABU-BAKR was not given preference because of much praying, fasting, and alms-giving. He was revered because of what was in his heart.*

What the Prophet meant by this is that Abu-Bakr's superiority over others was not because of his great praying and fasting but because of the divine favor he enjoyed. And that favor was God's love.

On Resurrection Day, the prayers, fasts, and alms-giving of each will be brought forward and placed in the balance, but when love is brought it won't even fit in the scale. So the most important thing is love. Now, when you see love in yourself, help it to increase and grow. When you see in yourself "capital," which is the urge to seek, increase it by continuously seeking, as it is said, "Blessing is in work." If you don't increase your capital, you will lose it.

[*Fihi ma Fihi*: Discourse 60]

---

* This is a hadith (*má fuddila abû-bakr . . .*). See al-Ghazali, *Ihya*, i, 40 (*juz'* i, *bâb* ii). Abu-Bakr was a close companion of the Prophet Muhammad. He was known for his sincerity, devotion, and generosity, and was one of the most observant of the faith. His generosity and love continually increased. He became the leader of the Muslim community, the first of the "Rightly Guided Imams," after the passing of Muhammad (may peace and blessings be with them).

The Poison of Pride

If little by little you don't run away from this worldly fortune,
autumn will come over this spring of yours.
East and West have seen many like you,
whose heads have been severed from their bodies.
After all, how should East and West,
which are impermanent, make anyone enduring?

You take pride in the fact that people, out of fear and bondage,
have become your flatterers for a few days.
When people bow in adoration to anyone,
they are really cramming poison into his soul.
Not until his adorer turns away from him,
does he realize how poisonous and destructive it was to him.

It's a blessing for the ego to be humbled!
Alas for the one who rose into a mountain of arrogance.
Know that pride is a killing poison,
fools are intoxicated by that poisonous wine.
When an unhappy wretch drinks such poison,
his head is delighted for a moment,
but soon enough the poison affects his spirit.

[*Mathnawi* IV: 2740–2747]

If you sat with anyone and felt agitated,
and the worries of your life did not disappear,
be careful, avoid their company,
for the souls of the dear ones will not forgive you.

[*Divan-e Shams-e Tabrizi:* Quatrain 423]

Climbing the Ladder of Egoism

Safety lies in poverty: dive into poverty.
The mountain that held some cash in its mine
was torn to pieces by the strokes of the pick.
The sword is for one who has a high and proud neck;
no blow falls on a shadow prostrate on the ground.

This egoism is the ladder climbed by creatures—
they must fall from this ladder in the end.
The higher anyone goes, the more foolish he is,
for his bones will be broken all the worse.

[*Mathnawi* IV: 2757–2759; 2763–2764]

The dominion which the vulgar have given to you,
they will take back from you as a debt.
Give up to God the dominion held on loan,
that He may bestow on you
the dominion to which all consent.

[*Mathnawi* IV: 2777–2778]

Trial by Fire

When a base and a genuine coin boast,
saying to each other,
"You are base; I am good and valuable,"
fire is the final test—
drop these two rivals into the fire.

Then the vulgar and the elect
will come to know their real state
and will move from opinion and doubt
to certain knowledge.

[*Mathnawi* IV: 2856–2858]

Between man and God there are only two veils,
health and wealth;
and all others arise from these two.
A healthy person will say: "Where is God?
I don't know where He is. I can't see Him."
Yet this very same person, when troubled by pain or sickness,
will begin to cry out, "O God! O God!"
and will confide his intimate secrets to Him.
So you see that health was veiling that man from God,
who was concealed beneath the threshold of pain.
So long as a man has wealth and possessions,
he can satisfy his wants and occupy himself day and night,
but the moment destitution rears its head
this same person's soul falls feeble,
and he turns to God.

[*Fihi ma Fihi*: Discourse 69]

The unbeliever's argument is just this,
that he says, "I see no place of abiding except this external
    world."
He never reflects that, wherever there is anything external,
that object gives information of hidden wise purposes.
The usefulness of every external object is, indeed, internal:
it is latent, like the beneficial quality in medicines.

[*Mathnawi* IV: 2878–2880]

If every heart could hear the Divine revelation,
why would there exist in the world any words and sounds?
That which is the very essence of grace to the vulgar
may seem like wrath to the close friends of God.

The coarse have to go through great pain and difficulty
to become able to perceive the difference,
because, O companion within the Cave,
from the perspective of one united with Him
these go-between words are only thorns, thorns, thorns.

Much tribulation, pain, and waiting are needed
for a pure spirit to be saved from words—
some people become more deaf, more stony,
while some become purified and rise in the Light.

[*Mathnawi* IV: 2982–2986]

The Qur'an Is Like a Shy Bride

THE QUR'AN IS like a shy bride. Even though you pull aside her veil, she won't show her face to you. The reason you have no pleasure or discovery in all your study of it is that it rejects your attempt to pull off its veil. It tricks you and shows itself to you as ugly, as if to say, "I am not that beauty." It is capable of showing any face it wants. If you do not tug at the veil and let go, but give water to its sown field, do it service from afar and try to do what pleases it, it will show its face to you, without you pulling aside its veil. Seek the people of God, *enter among my servants; and enter my paradise* [89:29–30].

God does not speak to just anyone, just as kings in this world do not speak to every weaver. They appoint viziers and deputies through whom people can reach them. God, also, has selected a certain servant, so that whoever seeks God can find Him through that servant. All the prophets have come for the sole reason that they are the Way.

[*Fihi ma Fihi*: Discourse 65]

Questioning is half of knowledge;
not everyone knows how to ask.
Both question and answer come from knowledge,
just as thorn and rose arise from earth and water.
Both eternal loss and freedom unfold from some knowledge,
as both the bitter and sweet fruit from watering.
Both hatred and love arise from some familiarity,
and from good food can develop both sickness and strength.
God's pen, Moses, became like an unknowing questioner
so that he might give the ignorant an inkling of the Mystery.
Let us, too, pretend we don't know,
and seek the answer.

[*Mathnawi* IV: 3008–3013]

The creation of the creatures of the world has a purpose—
become manifest,
so that the treasury of Divine gifts might not remain hidden.
God said, "I was a Hidden Treasure": pay attention!
Don't let your true substance be lost: become who you are!

[*Mathnawi* IV: 3028–3029]

By the Door of the Prophet

273

A prophet has come to earth:
you can grasp what you are longing for through him.
If you seek priceless pearls, *enter the houses by their doors.*
Keep knocking with the door-ring and wait:

your route is not directly to heaven—
you needn't take such a long road.

We have given to one of this earth the secrets of the mystery.
If you're not unfaithful, come, join with him.
Even though you may be a dry, hollow reed,
with his help you'll become sweet sugarcane.

[*Mathnawi* IV: 3326–3330]

Inseparable

O Beloved, we are locked in friendship with You.
Wherever You may step, we are the ground for You.
In the religion* of love it isn't allowed
to see the world through You and not see You.

[*Divan-e Shams-e Tabrizi:* Quatrain 870]

---

* *Madhab*, a school of Islamic jurisprudence.

Don't take charge, since you're not self-sufficient, no—
you're the student of the heart, made to learn from it.
Go to the heart, go, for you're really a part of it—
pay attention, for you are the servant of a good King.

To be His slave is better than to be a ruler;
didn't Iblis claim "*I am better*"?* O prisoner,
see the difference and choose
the servanthood of Adam, not the pride of Satan.

The one who is the Sun of the Way said,
"Good (*túbá*) comes to everyone whose ego bows low!"
Behold the shade of the Túbá tree of Paradise and lie down;
lay your head in that shade and rest without raising it.

If you go from this shade toward egoism,
you will soon become wayward and lose the way.
To be in the shade of one whose ego is humbled brings ease—
a place of rest for one who seeks spiritual purity.

[*Mathnawi* IV: 3340–3347]

---

* *Surah Sad* [38:76]. See also *Surah al-Hijr* [15:53].

A philosopher on his deathbed confessed:
"Compelled by acuteness of mind we galloped in vain.
In delusion we drew scornfully away from holy men
and swam instead in the sea of fantasy."

In the spiritual Sea swimming is useless:
there is no saving grace but the ark of Noah.
And so that king of the prophets said,
"I am the ship in this universal Sea,
or that person who, out of respect for my clear seeing,
has become my true representative instead of me."

We saints are the ship of Noah in the Sea,
so that you might not turn your face away from the ship.
Go not, like Canaan, to every mountain:
hear from the Qur'an the warning,
"*There is nothing that will protect you today.*"*

In your clouded sight, you turn away from the ship,
while the mountain of intellect seems like high ground.
Beware, beware! Don't regard this "low" with contempt:
pay attention to the grace of God that is attached to it.
Don't pay attention to the height of the mountain of thought,
for a single wave can turn it upside down.

[*Mathnawi* IV: 3355–3364]

---

* *Surah Hud* [11:43].

A person of good qualities knows right now
what will happen in twenty years.
That God-conscious person sees not only his own destiny—
he sees that of every creature of West and East.

The Light settles deeply within his eye and heart—
Why? Out of love of Home.
He is like Joseph, who dreamed of the sun and the moon
bowing in worship before him—
more than ten years later it came to pass.

The saying "He sees by the Light of God" is true.
The Divine Light splits the sky apart.
You don't yet have that Light in your eye—
you've traded real seeing for bodily senses.

The weakness of your vision reaches only as far as your foot—
you're weak and so is your guide.
Your eye is intended to be your guide, for hand and foot,
to discern right from wrong and where to take a step.

[*Mathnawi* IV: 3395–3403]

Even though God doesn't nod His head at you,
He gives you an inner delight
worth more than two hundred gestures of approval.
Anyway, that's how Intellect and Spirit give a nod:
if you sincerely serve the Loving Mind,
that's how it acknowledges your service—
your virtue grows.

God doesn't nod a head outwardly to you,
but He makes you a prince above worldly princes.
Secretly God gives you such strength
that worldly people bow down in front of you.
In the same way He gave to a stone such worth,
that it, too, was honored by His creatures—
it became pure gold.

If a mere drop of water gains God's favor,
it becomes a pearl and wins a higher rank than gold.
This body is just earth,
but when God gave it a spark of His Light,
it became like the moon,
and gained power over the world.
But be careful! The empire of this world,
though alluring, is really just a lifeless image.
Its enticing eye leads many foolish ones astray—
it seems to wink at you,
but only fools put their trust in it.

[*Mathnawi* IV: 3484–3493]

Inability

I am unable to give the secrets away.
I'm unable to show anything appropriate.
Something inside keeps me happy,
but I can't put my finger on it.

[*Divan-e Shams-e Tabrizi:* Quatrain 1236]

Muhammad counseled us, saying,
"Don't try to discern the Essence of God."
When you form ideas about His Essence,
you're just speculating.
It's not really God's Essence you're beholding—
it's only your own opinions soaring.
On the way to God there are a hundred thousand veils.
By nature, we all cling to some veil
while thinking we are truly seeing Him.
That's why the Prophet outlawed such false ideas,
to save us from useless imagination.

One whose conception of God lacks reverence
is doomed to fall on his face.
To fall on your face is to fall head first
while still thinking you're higher,
like a drunk who can't distinguish earth from heaven.

Witness His wonders—lose yourself in awe.
When one beholds the wonders of God,
abandoning pride and the claims of the ego,
contemplating His work, you find your true station
and fall into silence concerning the Maker.
Then you will only say from the depths of your soul,
"I cannot praise You enough."

[*Mathnawi* IV: 3700–3709]

A little ant saw a pen writing on a piece of paper,
and told another ant about that mystery,
saying, "The pen made such wonderful pictures
like sweet basil and beds of roses and lilies."
The other ant said, "The real artist is the finger;
the pen is just the instrument and sign."
A third ant said, "It's really the work of the arm
whose strength helps the slender finger draw."

In this way the argument was carried up the ranks
until a chief of the ants, who was a little bit wise,
said, "This accomplishment does not
come from the body that falls asleep or dies.
The bodily form is like a garment, or a staff—
bodies only move by means of intelligence and spirit."

That wise ant was still unaware
that without God's masterful influence
even intellect and heart would be inert.
If for a single moment His grace is withdrawn,
the skillful intellect stumbles and falls.

[*Mathnawi* IV: 3721–3729]

How Wrath Becomes Tender

Be only dumbfounded and distraught, nothing else,
so that God's help might come from every direction.
When you have become bewildered and crazed,
reduced to nothing,
you have begged with mute eloquence, *"Lead us!"**

The stringency of God is mighty,
but when you begin to tremble,
that mighty wrath becomes tender and gentle,
because the mighty Face is for terrifying the unfaithful;
but when you've become helpless,
it's all mercy and kindness.

[*Mathnawi* IV: 3751–3754]

---

* *Surah al-Fatiha* (The Opening), [1:5].

WHAT DOES NOT come into man's imagination is called a "gift," because whatever passes through his imagination is in proportion to his aspiration and his capacity. However, God's gift is in proportion to God's capacity. Therefore, the gift is that which is worthy in relation to God, not what is worthy in relation to the imagination or ambition of God's servant. "What no eye has seen nor ear heard nor has occurred to the mind of man"*—that is, "no matter how much eyes have seen, ears heard, or minds conceived the gift you expect of Me, My gift transcends it all."

[*Fihi ma Fihi*: Discourse 31]

---

* This is a *hadith qudsi* (*a'dadtu li-'ibâdî . . .*), "What no eye . . . have I prepared for my righteous servants." See *FAM* 93, no. 264.

Gabriel Embraces a Friend

The angel Gabriel unfurled
just a little of the awesome majesty
by which a mountain could be crumbled to dust.

A single royal wing of his covered both east and west.
Muhammad grew senseless in awe.

When Gabriel saw that senselessness,
how in astonishment his senses flew away,
he came and drew him into his arms.

That awe is the portion of strangers,
but this gentle affection comes to embrace a friend.

[*Mathnawi* IV: 3768–3771]

The Law is like learning about alchemy
from a teacher or a book;
the Path is like the transformative process,
like rubbing copper on the philosopher's stone;
the Truth is like the reality of copper turned to gold.
Those who know *about* alchemy
rejoice in their knowledge of it—
they say, "We know the theory well";
and those who practice it rejoice in their practice of it—
they say, "We do this work";
and those who have experienced the reality
rejoice in that reality—
they say, "We have become gold;
now we're delivered from theory and practice—
God has set us free."
*Each party is rejoicing in what they have** . . .

The Law is knowledge, the Path action,
the Truth attainment to God.
Then whoever hopes to meet his Sustainer, let him do good works
and associate none other in the service of his Lord.†
And God bless the best of His creatures,
Muhammad, and his Family and his Companions
and the people of his House, and grant them peace!

[*Mathnawi* V: Introduction]

---

* *Surah al-Mu'minun* (The Faithful), [23:53].
† *Surah al-Kahf* (The Cave), [18:10].

Greed is like the duck,
because her bill is always busy in the ground,
seeking what is buried in mud or dust.
Her throat is never idle;
the only Divine command she hears is "*Eat ye!*"
She's like a thief who turns the house upside down
and quickly fills his bag,
stuffing it with pearls and chickpeas, good or bad,
hastily cramming dry and wet into the same sack,
in fear of being caught.
Time presses, the opportunity is small, he's terrified:
as quick as he can he heaves the sack under his arm.
He has no faith in his Sovereign,
to believe that no enemy will be able to approach.

The faithful one, trusting in the One Who Gives Life,
conducts his raid in a leisurely manner and with care.
He has no fear of missing his chance or of any other threat—
he sees the King's power over any enemy.
He's not afraid of his fellow servants
coming to push him around or taking advantage—
he's seen the King's justice restraining his followers,
so that no one dares do violence to another.
He doesn't hurry and is calm—
he has no fear of missing his portion.
He carefully considers, with much patience and forbearance;
he is content, unselfish, and pure-hearted.
This consideration is a ray of the All-Compassionate One,
while that haste is Satan's nudging.

[*Mathnawi* V: 46–59]

They say, "Is there play after eighty?"
I say, "Is there play before eighty?"*

God, by His grace, bestows on the aged a youthful passion the
young cannot know. Such youthfulness refreshes, causing one to
leap and laugh, and gives one a desire to play. Because the elder
sees the world as new and is not weary of it, he desires to play—
he leaps and bounds, and grows robust.

"Great is the glory of old age if, when gray hairs appear,
one's steed of playfulness leaps wildly."

[*Fihi ma Fihi*: Discourses 33 and 34]

---

* This verse is anonymous. See Ibn Qutayba, '*Uyun al-akhbar*, iv, 53, line 6.

Whoever likes to eat clay goes for the dregs,
but the Sufi goes straight for the essence.
He says to himself, "The dregs must be essentially pure:
by following this clue the heart advances to purity."
The dregs are difficulty and their essence is ease:
the pure essence is like the ripened date,
and the dregs are the date when it's raw and bitter.
With every difficulty comes ease*; come, don't despair—
through death there is a way to Life.

When the Spirit displays its beauty without this body,
I cannot express the loveliness of that union.
When the Moon displays its radiance without this cloud,
it's impossible to describe such majesty and glory.
How delightful is that Kitchen full of honey and sugar,
of which these worldly rulers are just licking the platters!
How delightful is that haystack in the spiritual field,
of which every other stack is just picking up straws!
How delightful is the Sea of contented Life,
of which the Seven Seas are just a drop of dew!

[*Mathnawi* V: 358–361; 385–389]

---

* *Surah al-Inshirah* (The Opening Up of the Heart), [94:5].

The Divine Reality is with whoever is
the kernel emerged from the shell.
The Revelation says: *It's no crime to be blind,*
but don't let that stop you—
purify yourself with patience.
The medicine of patience will remove
the cataracts from your eyes,
and clear your heart for knowledge.

[*Mathnawi* II: 69–71]

The Loving-kindness of God Flies to the Broken

I am the devoted slave of one who will not sell his existence
except to that bountiful and generous Sovereign,
so that when he weeps, heaven begins to weep,
and when he moans in supplication,
the whole celestial sphere begins to cry, "O Lord!"

I am the devoted slave of that high-aspiring copper
that humbles itself to nothing but the Elixir.
Lift up in prayer a broken hand—
the Loving-kindness of God flies toward the broken.

[*Mathnawi* V: 490–494]

IF YOU PLANT only the kernel of an apricot pit, nothing will grow; but if you plant it together with its shell, it will grow. From this we realize that external form also has a purpose. Prayer is internal: "There is no prayer without the presence of the heart."* However, you must bring it into external form, with physical bowings and prostrations. Only then do you gain full benefit and reach your goal.

Those ... who persevere in their prayers [70:23]. This refers to the prayer of the spirit. The prayer of form is temporary; it is not continual. The spirit of this world is an endless ocean; the body is just the shore and dry limited land that is finite. So, continual prayer belongs only to the spirit. The spirit also has a kind of bowing and prostration; however, bowing and prostrating must be manifested in external form because there is a connection between substance and form, and unless they come together, there is no benefit.

[*Fihi ma Fihi*: Discourse 38]

---

* The hadith (*lâ salât . . .*) is given in *FAM* 5, no. 10.

He Alone Is Their Wages

Since the Divine has given the command "*Refrain yourselves,*"*
there must be some desire from which you need to turn your face.
And so the command "*Eat*" is for the sake of the trap of appetite;
after that comes "*Do not exceed*"—that is self-control.
Without the pain of self-restraint, no recompense arrives.
How admirable is that self-restraint
and how joyful is that recompense,
such recompense that charms the heart
and increases the life of spirit!
For God's lovers He alone is all their joy and sorrow;
He alone is their wages—they work for Him.
If they look at anything but the Beloved, it's not love,
it's only idle passion.

[*Mathnawi* V: 581–587]

---

* *Surah Baqarah* (The Cow), [2:35]. All three of these Qur'anic references refer
to the moment of Adam being tempted in the Garden.

Wonderful! Is there any beauty
but from His reflection?
This body moves only through spirit.
With a faulty spirit a body will never become sweet,
even though you pour honey all over it.
You already know this, if for one day
you have been spiritually alive
and have been granted a cup
from the Soul of the soul.

[_Mathnawi_ V: 592–594]

The Beautiful Feathers

Don't in a moment of desire
destroy the face of contentment,
and don't mar humility's sweet face with pride.
Don't distort the face of generosity with your greed,
and don't by leaning toward the ego,
compromise the fair face of worship.
Don't tear out the feathers
that belong to Paradise—
don't tear out those feathers
that allow you to journey on the Way.

[*Mathnawi* V: 610–612]

SOMEONE SAID, "We have come to know each and every condition of humankind. Not a bit of the condition and nature of the human being or his hot and cold humors has escaped us. Yet it has not been ascertained what part of him will abide forever."

If that could be known merely by words, then such effort and exertion would not be necessary, and no one would have to go through such pain and effort to discover it. It is like someone who comes to the seashore and sees nothing but turbulent water, crocodiles, and fish. He says: "Where are the pearls they speak of? Perhaps there are no pearls." How can one obtain a pearl just by looking at the sea? Even if he measures out the sea cup by cup a hundred times, he won't find a pearl. One must be a diver in order to discover pearls; and not every diver will find them, only a fortunate, skillful one.

The sciences and arts are like measuring the sea with a cup; the way to finding pearls is something else. Many a person is adorned with every accomplishment and possessed of wealth and beauty but has nothing of this intrinsic meaning in him; and many a person is a wreck on the outside, with no fairness of feature, elegance, or eloquence, but within is found the intrinsic meaning that abides forever. It is that which ennobles and distinguishes the human being.

[*Fihi ma Fihi*: Discourse 50]

O You who make nitrous earth to become bread,
and O You who make dead bread to be life,
O You who make the distracted soul to be a guide,
and O You who make the wayless wanderer to be a prophet,
You raise a piece of earth to heaven,
and from the stars, You make the earth grow fertile.

The eye of the heart that contemplates the firmament
perceives the continual alchemy that is here.
From the day when you came into existence,
you were fire or air or earth.
If you had remained in that condition,
how would you have reached such heights?
The Transmuter did not leave you in your first state:
He established a better state in the place of the former;
and so on till He gave you a hundred thousand states,
one after the other, the second always better than the first.

Consider change as coming from the One Who Transmutes;
ignore the intermediaries—
if you pay attention to them,
you'll only distance yourself from their Origin.
It's your bewilderment that brings you into the Divine Presence.
You have gained all these lives from successive deaths:
why have you averted your face from dying in Him?

[*Mathnawi* V: 783–796]

The meanest earning that goes on in the world,
is it ever practiced without the guidance of a master?
It begins with knowledge and is followed by action
that it may yield fruit after a while or after death.
Apprentice yourself, O possessor of intelligence,
to a generous and righteous craftsman.
Seek the pearl in the oyster-shell, my brother,
and seek craftsmanship from the skilled.
If you meet sincere spiritual counselors,
deal fairly with them and be eager to learn:
don't put on any airs.
If a tanner wears a threadbare coat,
that doesn't diminish the master's mastery;
if the blacksmith with massive biceps
wears a patched apron while flexing the bellows,
his reputation doesn't plummet in people's eyes.
So strip the raiment of pride from your body:
in learning, put on the garment of humility.

[*Mathnawi* V: 1054–1061]

Water the Good Roots

You have scattered your awareness in all directions
and your vanities are not worth a bite of cabbage.
The root of every thorn
draws the water of your attention toward itself.
How will the water of your attention reach the fruit?
Cut away the harmful roots, cut them away.
Direct the water of God's Bounty to spirit and insight,
not to the knotted and broken world outside.

[*Mathnawi* V: 1084–1086]

"THE CITY OF YOUR DREAMS you found lacking nothing, except noble men." That city is the human being. If within him there are a hundred thousand accomplishments but not the intrinsic meaning, it would be better for that city to be in ruins. If it does have the intrinsic meaning, it doesn't matter if it has no external adornments—the *mysterion* must be there for it to flourish. In whatever state a human being may be, his *mysterion* is occupied with God, and his external preoccupations in no way hinder that inner occupation. In whatever state a pregnant woman may be—war or peace, eating or sleeping—the baby within her is growing, is being strengthened, and is receiving sensations within her womb without her even being aware of it. Humankind likewise is "pregnant" with that *mysterion. But the human being undertook [the faith]: truly he was unjust to himself, and foolish* [33:72], but God does not leave him in his injustice and foolishness. If out of the burden of physicality comes companionship, sympathy, and a thousand acquaintances, then consider what marvelous friendships and acquaintances will emerge from the *mysterion* to which the human being gives birth after death. It is like the root of a tree: although it is hidden from view, its effects are apparent on the branches.

[*Fihi ma Fihi*: Discourse 50]

Though Zulaikha shut the doors on every side,
still Joseph reached safety by making an effort.
Lock and door opened, and the way out appeared:
when Joseph put trust in God, he escaped.
Though the world has no visible exit door,
still one must run recklessly searching, like Joseph,
so that the lock may open and the door might appear,
so that the place of placelessness might become your home.

You came into the world, O afflicted one:
did you ever see the way that you came?
You came from a certain abode:
do you know how? No.
Even though you don't know,
beware of saying that there is no way:
by this wayless Way we all shall depart.

[*Mathnawi* V: 1105–1117]

When you have no sincerity,
at least don't presume to speak,
for words are mostly self-assertion—"we" and "I."
These words, retained in the heart,
are an income of spiritual kernels:
in silence the spiritual kernel grows a hundredfold.
When a word is spoken, the kernel is spent—
stop spending,
so that the ripening kernel might remain within you.
Someone who speaks little has strong thoughts:
when the husk, namely speech, becomes excessive,
the kernel shrinks.
When the rind is thick, the kernel is thin;
the rind thins when the kernel ripens well.
Pay attention to three fruits as they mature:
watch the walnut, almond, and pistachio.

[*Mathnawi* V: 1174–1179]

The king questioned someone, saying,
"In the end, what is inspiration,
or what is it a prophet has?"
He replied, "What is there indeed that he doesn't have,
or what fortune is there he has not attained?

Just for debate, I'll suppose that this prophetic inspiration
is not a treasurer of Divine revelations;
still, it's not less than the inspiration in the heart of the bee.
Since the words *God has inspired the bee**** arrived,
the dwelling of the bee has been filled with sweetness.
Through the Light of the inspiration of God
the Almighty and Glorious,
it filled the world with wax and honey.

This one who is the object of *We have honored the children of Adam*†
and is ever rising upward—
how should his inspiration be less than the bee's?"
Haven't you read the words *We have given Kawthar*?‡
Why, then, are you dry; why have you remained thirsty?

[*Mathnawi* V: 1236–1232]

---

* *Surah an-Nahl* (The Bee), [16:68].
† *Surah al-Isra'* (The Night Journey), [17:70].
‡ Kawthar is the eternal spring of Paradise.

Some have said that love causes servitude, but it is not so.
Rather, the beloved's wish is what causes servitude.

If the beloved wants the lover to serve,
servitude proceeds from the lover.
If the beloved doesn't want servitude,
the lover will cease being servile.

The abandonment of servitude does not nullify love.
Even if the lover performs no service, the love within him will.
Love is the root, and service is only the branch of love.

[*Fihi ma Fihi*: Discourse 62]

He Is Our Purchaser

In their desire for any sleazy purchaser,
people throw the real Purchaser to the winds.
He is our Purchaser—*God has purchased.**
Don't be so anxious for someone else to buy your goods.
Seek the Purchaser who is seeking you,
One who knows your beginning and your end.
Be careful, don't try to win every purchaser:
it's bad to make love to two sweethearts.
You will not get interest or capital from anyone else;
for sure, no one else could ever pay the price
of your reason and intellect.
He doesn't even have the price of half a horseshoe,
yet you are offering him something as precious as rubies.
The patiently persevering gain the true Purchaser,
because they haven't run vainly
toward just anyone who makes an offer.

[*Mathnawi* V: 1462–1470]

---

* *Surah at-Tawbah* (Repentance), [9:111].

The remedy for hardened hearts
is the gift bestowed by One who can transform.
Receptivity is not even needed for His bounty to arrive.
No, His bounty is needed so that you can receive—
bounty is the kernel and receptivity the husk.

[*Mathnawi* V: 1537–1538]

The Divine Throne is the source of justice and fairness:
beneath it are four rivers filled with forgiveness—
a river of milk, a river of everlasting honey,
a river of wine, and a river of clear water [47:15].
From the Throne they flow into Paradise,
and, finally, a little branch appears in this world, too.

But here those four rivers are muddied—by what?
By the toxins of loss and indigestion.
From each of those four rivers a sip has been poured
upon this dark earth, and a temptation has been offered,
so that the corrupt might seek its source;
but just a sip satisfies the worthless folk.

God has given milk and nourishment for infants:
He has made the breast of every mother a fountain of milk.
He has given wine to drive away grief and worry:
He has made of the grape a fountain to inspire courage.
He has created a fountain of honey inside the bee,
and made that sweetness a remedy for the ill.

He gave water universally to both high and low
for washing and for drinking.
All this so that you might follow the track
from these back toward their origin.
Don't be content with just this drop.

[*Mathnawi* V: 1628–1638]

The radiance of your face was not born from a pelvis, come.
Nor are you the design of some semen, come.
Don't hide within your anger,
because the beauty you are cannot be disguised, come.

[*Divan-e Shams-e Tabrizi:* Quatrain 2]

"THE BEST WORDS are those that are few and to the point." The best words are those that are beneficial, not that are many. *Say, God is one God* [112:1]: although these words are few in form, they are preferable to the long chapter *Surah Baqarah* [2] by virtue of being to the point. Noah preached for a thousand years, and forty people joined him. It is well known how long the Prophet preached, and yet so many regions had faith in him, and so many saints arose because of him. So, "much" and "little" are not criteria; the important thing is conveying the meaning. Some people's few words can be more to the point than other people's many words—like an oven. Just as when the fire in an oven gets too hot you can't use it or even get close to it; yet you can use a weak lamp in a thousand ways. So it is obvious that the important thing is being of benefit. For some people it is more beneficial to see than to hear. If they hear words, it could harm them.

A shaikh from India set out to see a great mystic. When he reached the door of the shaikh's cell in Tabriz, a voice came from inside the cell, saying: "Go back. It is beneficial enough for you to have come to the door. If you see the shaikh it will harm you."

A few words that convey meaning are like a lighted lamp that kisses an unlit lamp and departs. That is enough for it; it reaches its goal.

A prophet is not his form; a prophet's form is his steed. A prophet is love and affection, and that is what remains forever. Similarly, the form of Salih's camel was that of a camel; the prophet is that true love and affection that are eternal.

[*Fihi ma Fihi*: Discourse 63]

The mystic Abu Yazid, may God sanctify his spirit, said,
"During all these years I have never spoken to any creature
or heard any creature speak to me;
but people fancy that I am speaking and listening to them,
because they do not see the Most Great Speaker,
of whom they, in relation to me, are just the echo."
The intelligent hearer pays no heed to the echo.
There is a well-known proverb to this effect:
"The wall said to the nail, 'Why are you splitting me?'
The nail replied, 'Look at the one who is hitting me.'"

[*Mathnawi* V: Introduction to section 1683]

In the hope of journeying upward, arise
and stand steadfast within the sanctuary,*
pray and weep like a candle, O youth!
Let your tears fall like rain,
and burn ardently in aspiration all night long,
like the candle beheaded by the flame.
Close your lips to food and drink,
and come quickly toward this Heavenly feast.

[*Mathnawi* V: 1728–1730]

---

* Literally: "before the *mihrab.*" The word *mihrab* (the prayer-niche of a mosque indicating the direction of prayer) means "sanctuary." It is also a metaphor for the heart.

LOVERS HAVE HEARTACHES which no medicine can cure, neither sleeping, nor wandering, nor eating. The only cure is seeing the Beloved. "Meeting the friend is mending the sickness."

This is so true that if a hypocrite sits with the faithful, he will be influenced by them and immediately become one of faith; as God says, *"When they meet those who have faith, they say, 'We have faith'"* [2:14]. How then must it be when one of the faithful sits with one of the faithful? Consider what benefits must be conferred!

Consider how wool is turned into a patterned carpet by proximity with an intelligent person. See how earth can be turned into a fine palace by being in connection with someone intelligent. If association with the intelligent has such an effect on inanimate objects, think what effect association of one who is faithful with another faithful one will have. Inanimate objects are elevated to such a level through association with the partial soul and intellect. If all this is a shadow of the partial intellect, and one can deduce a person from his shadow, then deduce what intellect and reason is needed to produce the heavens, the sun and moon, the seven layers of earth, and all that lies between. All these existing things are shadows of the Universal Intellect. Just as the shadow of the partial intellect is proportionate to the shadow of its person, the shadow of the Universal Intellect, which is all existing things, is proportionate to That.

[*Fihi ma Fihi*: Discourse 63]

A Real Gem

Until the gem surrendered itself,
when did it ever become a jewel set into a ring?

To keep being stony
and to say "I" is crazy—
it's time for you to die to self; let go.

Pride always grasps after power and riches
because the bath-furnace burns perfectly with dung.

These two nurses just plump up the skin—
they stuff it with fat and flesh and arrogance and pride.

They focus on the shell, thinking it's the kernel;
they don't raise their eyes to the kernel of the kernel.

[*Mathnawi* V: 1945–1949]

If you have just come from the fountain,
why are you thirsty?
And if you are the gland of the musk deer,
then where is the fragrance of musk?
How is there no trace in you
of that which you speak and describe,
O exalted one?

A certain man asked a camel,
"Hey, where are you coming from,
O you whom fortune attends?"
He replied, "From the hot-bath in your street."
Said the other, "Truly, that's apparent
from the state of your knees!"

[*Mathnawi* V: 2438–2441]

The Master of the Stable is one thing and the ass another:
not everyone who has entered the stable is an ass.
But why are we talking about asses?

Let's talk about the rose garden and fresh roses,
and the pomegranate and the citron and the apple branch,
and the wine and the countless fair maidens,

or speak of the sea whose waves are pearls
and whose pearls can also speak and see,
or of the birds that pick roses

and lay eggs of silver and gold,
or of the falcons who nurture partridges
and fly both with their bellies turned downward
and also on their backs.

In the world there are invisible ladders,
leading step by step up to the summit of Heaven.
There is a different ladder for every class,
there is a different heaven for every traveler's way.

[*Mathnawi* V: 2550–2557]

Go Easy on the Lovers

Stop judging the lovers;
see them with the eyes of love.
Their time is precious
and their souls are watching out
for the Beloved:
in that moment they can't make excuses to you.
Apprehend what's going on within them,
don't judge them by their words;
don't wound the hearts of lovers.
Do you see how you condemn their enthusiasm?
We're not saying, "Abandon all prudence";
yes, be cautious, but give allowance;
sometimes it's better not to interfere.

[*Mathnawi* V: 2767–2771]

I and My Broken Heart

For me the gate of union has been closed by the Friend.
My heart has been broken by the sorrow and pain of the Friend.
From now on I and my broken heart will wait at the gate,
for those with a broken heart have the favor of the Friend.

[*Divan-e Shams-e Tabrizi:* Quatrain 245]

Seek refreshment from the Sacred Chalice
whose wine leaves you selfless and free of will.
Then all volition will belong to that wine,
and your drunkenness can be excused.
Whatever you touch will be touched by the wine;
whatever you sweep away will be swept away by the wine.

The drunkard who has sipped wine from this Chalice—
how could he do anything but justice and goodness?
You no longer care what your hands and feet do,
for they are under the influence of the Wine of Oneness.

[*Mathnawi* V: 3105–3110]

Every body resembles a bowl or a pot,
containing both food and heartache.
The bowl is seen, the contents hidden—
only the one who tastes knows what is gained from it.
The form of Joseph was a cup of extraordinary beauty:
from it his father drank a hundred exhilarating wines,
but his brothers took poisoned water from it
that increased their hatred and anger.
For Zulaikha the drink she took was sweet as sugar—
she drank a different intoxicant from the hand of Love.
The nourishment that came from Joseph to that fair one
was again different than that which came to Jacob.
The sherbets are varied though the bowl is one,
so that you may have no doubt
concerning the wine of the Unseen.
The wine belongs to the Unseen, the bowl to this world—
you can see the bowl, but the wine within is quite hidden:
very hidden from the eyes of the uninitiated,
but clearly visible to the adept.

[*Mathnawi* V: 3298–3306]

Is there any one person who is worth a thousand others?
The Saint. Actually, that servant of the Most High
equals a hundred generations.

The great rivers kneel before the jug
that has a channel to the sea, especially this Sea of Reality;

for all the other seas, when they heard
this royal command and mighty cry—

their mouths became bitter with shame and confusion
because the Greatest Name had been joined with the least.

At the coming together of this world
with the world beyond, this world shrinks in shame.

Anything I can say falls short, for what resemblance exists
between the coarse and the most fine?

Just because the crow caws in the orchard,
why should the nightingale stop its sweet song?

Everyone, then, has his own customer
in this bazaar of *He does what He pleases.**

[*Mathnawi* VI: 22–29]

---

* *Surah al-Imran* [3:37].

The dessert provided by the briar patch
is nothing more than a morsel for the fire.
The fragrance of the rose
is food for the intoxicated brain.

The filth that we find repulsive,
to the pig and the dog is a delicious treat.
If the filthy go cavorting in the dirt,
still the clear waters move to purify.

Though snakes are scattering venom
and though the sour-faced distress us,
still the bees in their mountain hives
keep depositing sweet stores of honey.

[*Mathnawi* VI: 30–34]

JESUS WAS ASKED, "O Spirit of God, what is the most tremendous and most difficult thing in this world and the next?"

"The wrath of God," he answered.

"What can save us from it?" they asked.

"Curb your anger; restrain your wrath," he replied.

The way to do this is to oppose the self and, when it wants to complain about something, give thanks instead. Exaggerate it so much that love is generated within you, for to give false thanks is to seek love from God.

So says our great master [Muhammad]: to complain of a creature is to complain of the Creator. He has also said that enmity and anger are hidden within you, from you, like fire. When you see a spark leap out of this fire, put it out right away, so that it may return to non-existence from whence it came. If you help it along with the match of a word of recrimination or retort, it will find a way to come again out of non-existence and only with difficulty will you be able to send it back.

Repel your enemy with something better, so that you may vanquish him: your enemy is not his flesh and bone, it is his evil thought. When that is repelled from you by means of abundance of gratitude, it will be repelled from him also. This occurs naturally; as the saying goes, "The human being is a slave to beneficence."

[*Fihi ma Fihi*: Discourse 68]

Our war and our peace is within the Light of Essence—
it's not ours alone, it's all between the two fingers of God.
War of nature, war of action, war of speech—
this terrible conflict goes on among all parts.
The world is maintained by means of this struggle:
consider the elements, so the problem might be solved.
The four elements are four strong pillars
that support the roof of the apparent world.

Each pillar is a destroyer of the other:
the pillar known as water is a destroyer of the flames.
The edifice of this world is based on opposites—
for better or worse we are at war.
My states of mind and body are mutually opposed:
each one has a mutually opposite effect.
Since I am incessantly waylaying myself,
how should I act in harmony with someone else?

Witness the surging armies of my "states,"
each struggling with the other.
Contemplate the same grievous war inside yourself—
why, then, do you keep battling with others?
Or is it because you have no way out
unless God redeems you from this war
and brings you into the world with the single color of peace?
That world is nothing but everlasting and flourishing,
because it is not built from opposites.

[*Mathnawi* VI: 45–56]

There is a mystery to be told,
but where is an ear to listen?
Where is a parrot who wants such sugar?
For the elect parrots there is a profound candy:
a food the eyes of the vulgar parrots never see.

You will not taste that purity
just because you dress like a dervish.
It is a spiritual reality, not just *tadum tadum tadum.**

Jesus doesn't withhold candy from the ass,
but the ass is naturally pleased with straw.
If candy had roused delight in the ass,
Jesus would have poured out a hundred pounds for it.

Know that this is the meaning of the verse *We seal their mouths*†:
this knowledge is important for the traveler on the Way,
so that perhaps by his following
the Way of the Seal of the Prophets,
a heavy seal might be lifted from his lips.

[*Mathnawi* VI: 158–164]

---

* Not just the rhyming meters of poetry: *fa'úlun fá'ilát.*

† *Surah Ya Sin* (O Thou Human Being), [36:65]. *On that Day We shall set a seal on their mouths—but their hands will speak unto Us, and their feet will bear witness to whatever they have earned [in life].*

Iblis had knowledge, but he had no love,
and when God created Adam,
Iblis saw only a being of clay.

Though you may know all the facts and footnotes,
O esteemed professor, this will not open
the inner eyes that discern the invisible.

Most scholars only pay attention to turbans and beards:
they ask about the résumés and careers
of people they don't even know.

But you, O knower, have no need of such introductions:
you can see for yourself, for you are the rising Light.

All that really matters is sincerity,
consciousness of God and the Way,
the result of which is well-being in both worlds.

[*Mathnawi* VI: 260–264]

Fattening

An animal is made fat by fodder;
man is fattened by honor and eminence.
An animal is fattened through its gullet
and by what it gulps and chews;
man is fattened through his ear.

[*Mathnawi* VI: 290–291]

The One Who Knows

No matter what mask you wear, this King knows you.
Even if you cry out wordlessly, he knows.
Everybody wants to stand up and lecture—he knows.
I am the servant of the one who is silent.

[*Divan-e Shams-e Tabrizi:* Quatrain 642]

Lay the Burden on Yourself

Be a servant; be a horse someone can ride upon,
rather than a coffin others have to carry.

The selfish man wishes everyone to carry him:
they bring him, like a dead rider, to the grave.

If you dream of anyone being carried on a bier,
he will ride high in the stirrup of eminent office.

Just as the coffin is a burden on the people who carry it,
these bigshots have laid their burden
on others' shoulders.

Don't lay your burden on anyone; lay it on yourself:
do not seek eminence; it's best to be poor.

[*Mathnawi* VI: 324–329]

Desire Nothing from Anyone

There are things you desperately want now
that you will curse in the end, saying,
"You looked like a glamorous city,
but really you're a ruined village."

Turn away from that city of desires now,
before you end up unloading in the wilderness.
Renounce it now while you still possess a hundred gardens,
before you are completely lost in the tangle of desires.

The Prophet said, "If you desire Paradise from God,
desire nothing from anyone else.
When you desire nothing from anyone,
I am your guarantee for *the Garden* and the vision of God."

[*Mathnawi* VI: 330–334]

A man heard some footsteps in the night
and struck a match to light a lamp.
At the very same moment the unseen intruder
sat beside him in the dark,
and whenever the tinder caught fire,
he put it out with the tip of his finger,
so that the kindled flame might vanish.

The man thought it was dying by itself:
he couldn't see someone extinguishing it.
The man said, "Maybe this tinder was moist:
because of its dampness the flame keeps dying."
In such a murky darkness, he didn't see
that flame-extinguisher at his side.

So, too, the cynic's eye, because of its dimness,
doesn't see such a flame-extinguisher in his heart.
How is the heart of any conscious person
unaware that with everything that moves
there must be someone who is responsible for moving it?

[*Mathnawi* VI: 357–364]

Finally

Floodwaters all around the ruined abode of life
and the glass of life about to be filled,
but be happy, for after you blink your eyes
your baggage will be carried away by the Porter of Time.

[*Divan-e Shams-e Tabrizi:* Quatrain 922]

When the call comes to arise and depart,
your skill at arguing disappears,
and you catch sight of the world of silence.
Stop talking!
What a pity if you don't know inner silence!
Polish your heart for a day or two:
make that mirror your book of contemplation.
From seeing a reflection of the kingly Joseph
old Zulaikha grew young anew.
By the sun of July,
old winter's chill transforms to heat;
by Mary's burning sighs
a dry branch becomes a fruitful palm tree.

[*Mathnawi* VI: 1285–1290]

EVEN THOUGH SOMEONE may be heedless, others are not un-
aware of her. If you work hard pursuing things of this world, you
become heedless of your real concern. One must seek God's
contentment, not that of others, because contentment, love, and
affection are "on loan" in people, placed there by God. If He so
desires, He can withhold ease and contentment and then, even
with all the means of enjoyment, food, and luxury provided, ev-
erything becomes painful and a difficulty.

All these means are like a pen in the hand of God's omnipo-
tence. God is the mover and writer—until He wishes, the pen
doesn't move. Now you look at the pen and say, "There must be a
hand to this pen." You can see the pen, but you don't see the hand.
You see the pen, and then think of the hand.

Now how does what you see relate to what you say? The saints
are always seeing the hand and say that it needs a pen. They are so
focused on the beauty of the hand that they aren't concerned with
seeing the pen. So they simply say that it must be that such a hand
has a pen. You enjoy contemplating the pen so much you forget
about the hand. They so delight in the sweetness of contemplat-
ing the hand, how can they even think about the pen?

[*Fihi ma Fihi*: Discourse 63]

If you desire to be safe from harm,
close your eye to the beginning
and try to contemplate the end,
so that you may regard what doesn't yet exist
as really existent, and look upon all that exists,
so far as it is perceived by the senses,
as of small importance.

At least consider this, that everyone who possesses reason
is daily and nightly in quest of the relatively non-existent.

In begging, he seeks a gift that does not yet exist;
in the shops he seeks a profit that does not yet exist.
In the cornfields he seeks a crop that does not yet exist;
in the plantations he seeks a date-palm that does not yet exist.
In the colleges he seeks a knowledge that does not yet exist;
in the Christian monasteries
he seeks virtue that does not yet exist.
All these have thrown what does exist behind them
and are seekers of, and devoted to, what does not yet exist,

because the mine and treasury of God's doing
is not other than non-existence
in the process of being
brought into manifestation.

[*Mathnawi* VI: 1360–1367]

This heart of mine is like an orchard,
and my eyes are like the rain clouds:
when the clouds weep, the orchard laughs.

In a year of drought
the sun's laughter
throws the orchards into an agony of death.
You have read the words of revelation *and weep ye much**—
why do you keep grinning
like a roast sheep's head?

You will be the light of the house,
if like the candle you melt in tears.
The mother's or father's sour face
keeps the child from all kinds of harm.

You have experienced the pleasure of laughing.
Now, O excessive laugher,
experience the pleasure of weeping
and recognize that it is a mine of sugar.

Since thinking of Hell causes people to weep,
in that sense Hell is better than Paradise.
Within tears, find a hidden laughter;
seek treasure amid ruins, O sincere one.

[*Mathnawi* VI: 1579–1586]

---

* See *Surah at-Tawba* (Repentance), [9:82].

You are like an herb on a small hill—
your foot is planted in the earth,
but your head is tossed by the winds of desire.

Like the people of Moses in the heat of the desert,
you have stayed forty years in the same place.
Every day you march strenuously till nightfall,
yet you find yourself still
in the first stage of your journey.

You will never traverse this three hundred years' distance
as long as you let love for the golden calf stand in your way.
Until the illusion of the calf left their hearts,
the desert was a fiery whirlpool.

Besides this calf which you have obtained from God,
you've experienced infinite abundance and graces.
You have the nature of a cow—
because of your love for this calf
other blessings have run away from your heart.

Now, inquire of each part of yourself—
these dumb parts have a hundred tongues
to recount the bounties of the World-Provider
hidden in the pages of Time.

Day and night you keep eagerly seeking stories,
while every part of you
is telling you the story of His gifts.

[*Mathnawi* VI: 1787–1796]

Although the water boils,
the heat of the fire is hidden.
The froth of a thousand bubbles
is stirred by hidden fingers of fire.

In the same way, those intoxicated with union
are pregnant with ecstatic feelings and words.
Their mouths are gaping at the beauty,
while their eyes are withdrawn from this world.

Those spiritual progeny
are not made from these four elements;
that's why they are not seen by these eyes.
Born of illumination, they are covered by a pure veil.
We said "born," but in reality,
this expression is just a hint.

Hush, be silent, so that One may speak*—
the One who says, "Be," and it is.
Don't sing like a nightingale
to a rose as eloquent as this.
This rose has its own song and call—
hold your tongue, O nightingale, be all ear!

[*Mathnawi* VI: 1808–1816]

---

* Literally "the King of 'Say.'" The word *Qul* ("Say!") begins a number of verses
in the Qur'an, for instance, "Say, O Prophet . . ." It is through God that we come
into being and are caused to speak, as all the Most Compassionate and Powerful
Creator needs do is to say, "Be" and it is (*Kun fa yakun*) [36:82]. Through the
Divine "Word," everything comes into existence, and prophets and God's saints
are enabled to convey the fragrance of that Rose Garden.

When grief possesses you, if you are up to it,
you would question that moment of despair
and would say to it, "O Sorrow,
whose very presence denies the gifts
that Perfection has bestowed,
if the fresh gladness of Spring is not always yours,
is not your body still a storehouse of roses?

Since your body is a heap of roses,
your thought is like rosewater;
the rosewater denying the rose—
now that's truly amazing!"

To the one who apishly shows ingratitude,
even hay is withheld;
while sunshine and rain are lavished
on those who have a prophet's nature.

Being stubbornly ungrateful
is the rule followed by the ape,
while thankfulness and gratitude
is the way of the prophets.

[*Mathnawi* VI: 1824–1829]

Whenever, after crying out in his need,
the poor one reached exhaustion and despair,
he would hear from the Presence, "Come!"
This Maker is One who humbles and exalts:
without these two no work is done.
Consider the lowness of the earth and the loftiness of the sky:
both are needed for the heavens to whirl.

Consider the lowness and loftiness of this earth:
one half of the year it is barren,
the other half it is green and fresh.
And the lowness and loftiness of distressful Time:
half is day and half is night.
And the lowness and loftiness of this blended nature of ours:
sometimes healthy and sometimes crying out with illness.

Like this are all the changing conditions of the world—
famine and drought and peace and war;
this world flies like a bird in the air
by means of these two wings.
By these means every soul is tested by fear and hope.
So the world is always trembling like a leaf
as the winds of resurrection and death
blow off the desert or from the frigid north.

All this is so that the dying vat of our Jesus
may replace those hundred other dyes.
The world of Unity is like a salt mine—
whatever has fallen into it has taken on its color.

[*Mathnawi* VI: 1846–1856]

We are in love with love; Muslims are something else.
We are weak as an ant, and Solomon is something else.
Expect from us only paleness and spilled guts.
The bazaar of the linen merchants is something else.

[*Divan-e Shams-e Tabrizi:* Quatrain 225]

The Day of Reckoning is justice,
and justice consists in giving
to everyone what is proper:
the shoe belongs to the foot,
and the cap belongs to the head.
This is so that every seeker
may attain what he's searching for,
and that everything destined to set
may reach its point of setting.
Nothing the seeker seeks is withheld:
the sun is paired with heat
and the cloud with water.

[*Mathnawi* VI: 1887–1889]

THE GIST OF all this is that the world is like a mountain—whatever you say, good or evil, echoes off that mountain. If you were to imagine, "I made a sweet sound, but the mountain gave an ugly reply," that would be absurd. When a nightingale sings to the mountain, could it ever reply with the voice of a crow, a human, or a donkey? Know then for certain that it is you who made the donkey noise.

[*Fihi ma Fihi*: Discourse 40]

The hand of Moses took a radiance
from his bosom that surpassed
the moon in the dark night sky,
implying, "That which you sought
from the awesome celestial sphere has risen,
O Moses, from your own chest,
so that you may know
the heavens are the reflection
of the perceptive faculties of the human being."
Didn't the hand of Divine Glory
create Intelligence before all else,
even before the creation of the two worlds?
This discourse is clear to some
and exceedingly esoteric to others,
because a fly is not intimate with the Phoenix.

[*Mathnawi* VI: 1933–1937]

Fly Toward the Whole

If someone should puff at God's candle,
how could that candle be extinguished?
His cheeks and nose would be burned.
Bats often dream that this world
will be left orphaned by the Sun.

The fierce waves of the seas of the Spirit
are a hundred times as great
as those of the Flood of Noah.
Yet a hair got in Canaan's eye,
and he turned away from Noah and the ark
and fled to the imagined safety of a mountain.
Then half a wave swept Canaan and the mountain
into the abyss of disgrace.

The moon scatters her light and the dog barks:
how can a dog eat the light of the moon?
Those night-travelers who travel so swiftly with the moon,
why should they stop their journey
just because of barking dogs?
Straight like an arrow,
the part is flying toward the Whole.

[*Mathnawi* VI: 2082–2089]

The realized being* is the soul of religion and piety:
realization is the result of past discipline.
Austerity is the labor of sowing;
realization is the growth of the seed.

His struggle and steadfastness are like the body,
while the soul of this sowing is the growth and its harvesting.
He is both the command to do right and the right itself;
he is both the revealer of mysteries and that which is revealed.
He is our sovereign today and tomorrow—
the husk is forever a slave to his ripe kernel.

[*Mathnawi* VI: 2090–2094]

---

* The mature gnostic, *'árif*: the one who has realized and experienced the Divine Truth.

Drum and banner belong to the spiritual king;
anyone who calls him a parasite is an idiot.
The heavens serve his glowing moon;
East and West are begging him for bread.
*But for thee** should be inscribed on his seal:
everyone receives something from his grace.
If he did not exist, the heavens would not revolve,
nor would the angels have their home.
The seas teeming with life would not awe us,
nor offer up their treasure of pearls;
Earth would be without its treasures buried deep,
and without wildflowers and gardens of jasmine.
Our hunger is for the sustenance bestowed by him—
the fruits are dry-lipped, waiting for his rain.
Take note: in the Divine command to give alms
this knot is tied upside down—
give alms to him who gives alms to your self.
All your gold and silk comes to you
from the apparently poor man—
bestow alms on someone who is really rich,
O you who are really poor.

[*Mathnawi* VI: 2101–2109]

---

* "But for thee (O Prophet), I would not have created the world," is a Qur'anic theme.

That which is most real
is nearer than your jugular vein.
You've shot the arrow of thought far afield.

Despite all your bows and arrows,
the target is near, but you have shot too far.
The farther one shoots,
the farther one is from the treasure.

The philosopher just about killed himself with thinking—
let him run on in vain,
for he has turned his back to the treasure.

Let him run on: the more he runs, the farther he goes
away from the object of his heart's desire.

That Divine Being said, "... *those who have striven in Us,*"*
not, "... *those who have striven away from Us,*" O restless one.

[*Mathnawi* VI: 2353–2358]

---

* *Surah al-Hajj* (The Pilgrimage), [22:78] and *Surah al-Ma'idah* (The Feast),
[5:35]: *O you who have attained to faith, remain conscious of God, and strive to come
closer to Him, and strive hard in His cause, so that you might attain felicity.*

THE STORY IS TOLD of a teacher who was so poor that during the winter he had nothing to wear but a single cotton garment. By chance a rushing river had caught up a bear in the mountains and swept it down with its head hidden under the water. Some children saw the back of the bear and cried out: "Teacher, look! A fur coat has fallen into the water. Since you are cold, pull it out." The teacher was in such need and so cold that he jumped in to get the fur coat. The bear dug its claws into him and held him in the water. The children cried, "Teacher, bring the fur out or, if you can't, let it go and you come out!"

"I've let it go," he answered, "but it won't let go of me! What can I do?"

How then should yearning for God let you go? This is a cause for thanks—that we are not in our own hands but in God's. An infant knows nothing but milk and its mother. God does not leave it in that state but causes it to move to the stage of eating bread and playing. Then He draws it to the stage of reason. In relation to the other world we are just infants—this world is another mother's breast. God will not leave you until He brings you further, until you realize that this state is just infancy, nothing more.

[*Fihi ma Fihi*: Discourse 26]

Keep Your Eye on the Friend

When a friend is seated beside his Friend,
a hundred thousand tablets of mystery are opened.

The brow of the Friend is a Preserved Tablet*
where the secret of the two worlds appears.

The Friend is the guide on the way during his friend's journey:
so Muhammad said, "My Companions are like stars."

The star shows the way across desert sands and at sea:
fix your eye on the Star, for he is the one to be followed.

Keep your eye on his face:
don't stir up dust with discussions and arguments,

you'll just veil the Star with that dust.
The witnessing eye is better than the stumbling tongue.

Be silent so he may speak who calms the dust—
he whose inmost garment is Divine inspiration.

[*Mathnawi* VI: 2641–2647]

---

* "Preserved Tablet" (*lawhim mahfuz*): a term used to describe the Qur'an and
also as a metaphor for the heart of the saint.

Love is thirsting to drink
and seeks another with that thirst.
This Love and that lover
are at each other's heels,
like Day and Night.
Day is in love with Night
and has lost control of itself;
when you look inwardly,
you will see that Night
is even more in love with it.
Never for one instant
do they cease from seeking;
never for one moment
do they stop pursuing each other.
This one has caught the foot of that one,
and that one the ear of this one.
This one is distraught with that one,
and that one is beside itself for this one.
In the heart of the beloved
the lover is all that matters.

In the lover's heart you will find
nothing but the beloved:
there nothing keeps them apart.
These two bells are on one camel:
how could they ever think of
"Visit me once a week."
Did anyone ever pay
recurring visits to himself?

[*Mathnawi* VI: 2675–2683]

The Path of Reality

The light of *zikr** creates the full moon,
And brings those who are lost to the path of Reality.
At the times of the morning and evening *namaz,*†
make yourself a prayer, saying, *La illaha il Allah.*‡

[*Divan-e Shams-e Tabrizi:* Quatrain 11]

---

* *Zikr:* remembrance of God, often practiced as a chanted prayer, as well as silent absorption.
† *Namaz:* the Farsi word for the five-times-a-day ritual worship.
‡ *La illaha il Allah* ("There is no god but God"). This is often chanted as a *zikr.*

The troops of fantasy keep arriving,
tirelessly passing through the curtains of the heart.
If these ideas are not from one single Plantation,
how do they come so quickly, one after the other,
on each other's heels to the heart?
Company after company, the army of our ideas,
compelled by thirst,
rushes toward the fountain of the heart.
They fill their jugs and go—
continually, they appear and vanish.
Look at your thoughts as stars in the sky
revolving in the sphere of another heaven.
If you have experienced waves of beauty,
give thanks and do some good for others.
If you have experienced ill fortune,
give alms and ask God's pardon.
Who am I in relation to all this?
Come, O my Sovereign, make my ruling star auspicious;
turn toward me now.
Illumine my spirit with the Moon's light—
my soul is eclipsed by conjunction with the Dragon's Tail.*
Deliver it from vain imaginations and opinion,
deliver it from the dark well and tyrannous rope,
so that through Your good loving-kindness
this heart might lift its wings and soar
high above water and earth.

[*Mathnawi* VI: 2780–2789]

---

* The "dragon's tail" here refers to the "constellation" of the ego-self, whose actions are treacherous, compulsive, and dangerous.

The Endlessness of Knowledge

The sleep of the knower is better than worship,
if it is a knowing that brings awakening.

The quiet of the expert swimmer
is better than the exertion of one who can't swim.

Someone who can't swim keeps flailing and drowns,
while the good swimmer glides quietly onward.

Knowledge is an ocean without any shore—
the seeker of knowledge is a diver through the seas.

Though his life is a thousand years long,
he never wearies of seeking,

for as the Messenger of God has said,
"There are two greedy ones who are never satisfied:

the seeker of the apparent world
and the seeker of knowledge."

[*Mathnawi* VI: 3878–3883]

If you don't like the fragrance, don't come to our neighborhood.
And if you can't tear off your clothes, don't jump in the stream.
This is the direction from which all directions are directed.
Unless this is what you want, stay away from the center.

[*Divan-e Shams-e Tabrizi:* Quatrain 60]

The Beloved's Name

If Zulaikha piled up a hundred thousand names,
her meaning and intention always was Joseph.
When she was hungry, as soon as she spoke his name
she'd be filled with spiritual food
and drunk with his cup.

His name would quench her thirst—
the name of Joseph was a sherbet to her soul.
And if she were in pain, her pain would quickly
turn to blessing with his dear name.

In cold weather it was a fur to her.
This, this, the Beloved's name can do when one loves.
The vulgar keep saying the Holy Name,
but it doesn't do this work for them,
because their love isn't real.

The miracle Jesus fashioned by speaking the Name of *Hu**
came clearly to her through the name of Joseph.
When the soul is in union with God,
to speak of God is to speak of this soul,
and to speak of this soul is to speak of Him.

She was empty of self and filled with love for her friend,
and as the saying goes, "A pot drips what is in it."

[*Mathnawi* VI: 4033–4041]

---

* *Hu* is the pronoun of Divine Presence, the Name of God, spoken on the breath. By breathing this life into a lump of clay, Jesus transformed it into a living bird that flew.

The scent of the saffron of union brings laughter;
the smell of the onion of absence brings tears.
Most have a hundred objects of desire in their hearts,
but this isn't the way of love and affection.
Love's sun in the daytime is the Beloved's Face:
the sun is just a veil over that Face.
One who doesn't know the veil from the Face of the Beloved
is just a sun-worshipper: stay away from him.

The Beloved is both the lover's day and daily bread;
She is both the lover's heart and heartache.
God's fish receive from the Essence of the Water
their bread and water and clothes and medicine and sleep.
The lover is like a child drinking milk from the breast:
in the two worlds he knows nothing but milk.
The child knows that milk and yet doesn't know it—
intellectual ponderings have no means of entrance here.

This advertisement by Love made the spirit crazy
to find both the Opener and that which is opened by Her.
The spirit isn't mad to go on such a quest, no,
for it's the Sea Itself within it that carries it along,
not just a stream or a river.
How should the spirit find God?
One who finds God becomes lost in Her:
like a restless river he merges into the Ocean.
The seed becomes lost in the earth—
only then does it become a fig tree.

[*Mathnawi* VI: 4042–4053]

All selfish pleasures are a deceit and a fraud:
a lightning flash that is just a brief gleam,
false and fleeting, surrounded by darkness;
and your journey is long.

In a flash of lightning, you can neither read a letter
nor ride to your destination.
But, because you were enthralled by the lightning,
the beams of sunrise withdraw themselves from you.
Mile after mile through the night
the lightning's deception leads you on,
without a guide, through a dark wilderness.
On the mountain you stumble; you fall into a river—
you wander in this direction, and in that.

Filled with worldly ambitions, you'll never find the guide;
and if you find him, you will turn your face away,
saying, "I have traveled so far on this road,
and now this guide tells me I have lost my way.
If I follow his advice I must begin my journey
all over again under his authority,
but I have devoted my life to this journey:
I will go on, come what may."

Yes, you have journeyed far,
but only in opinion insubstantial as lightning:
come, make one tenth of that journey
for the sake of an inspiration
as glorious as sunrise.

[*Mathnawi* VI: 4094–4104]

The Ladder of Abraham

Abraham said, "O traveler, I will be your mighty bird;
when you make of me a ladder to journey aloft,
you will ascend to heaven without flying"—
as the heart, without provisions or riding-camel,
travels swiftly as lightning to west and east;
as man's consciousness, wandering abroad while he is asleep,
travels during the night to remote cities;
as the gnostic, sitting quietly in one place,
travels by an invisible path through a hundred worlds.

[*Mathnawi* VI: 4128–4132]

Profit and Loss

One word comes to the lips from Hell,
another word comes to the lips from the Spiritual City.
There is a spirit-increasing sea and a sea of distress:
these lips are where the two seas meet.
It's like a great market between two towns:
goods are brought there from all directions:
damaged, spurious, and deceptive commodities
and also worthwhile and precious things, like pearls.
The shrewdest traders in this market
carefully inspect all the wares.
To some this market is a place of profit,
while to others in their blindness it is a place of loss.
Every particle of the world, one by one,
is a swindle for the fool and deliverance for the wise.

[*Mathnawi* VI: 4281–4287]

If a child is in a state of foolishness and denial,
at any rate, thank God, he doesn't have much strength.
If a child is quarrelsome and mischievous,
thank God for his lack of power and skill.

But as for the childish undisciplined elder
who in his strength becomes an affliction to everyone—
when weapons and ignorance are brought together,
he becomes in his tyranny a world-consuming Pharaoh.

O poor one, thank God for your deficiency of means
that saves you from becoming an arrogant Pharaoh.
Give thanks to God that you are the oppressed, not
the oppressor, and secure from the temptations of power.

[*Mathnawi* VI: 4720–4725]

He is always pulling our ears, saying,
"*Do not lose hope!*"*

Although we are in a ditch
and overwhelmed by despair,
let's go dancing along, since He has invited us.

Let's dance along like spirited horses
galloping toward a familiar pasture.
Let's toss our feet, though no foot is there;
let's drain the cup, though no cup is there,

because all things there are spiritual:
it is reality upon reality upon reality.
Form is the shadow, reality is the sun.

[*Mathnawi* VI: 4742–4747]

---

* *Surah az-Zumar* (The Throngs), [39:53].

If I plant roses without You, nothing will grow but thorns.
And out of the eggs of hens, snakes will be born.
And if I take up the *rebab* without You, its strings will break.
If I try to play the melody of Eight Paradises, it becomes only four.

[*Divan-e Shams-e Tabrizi:* Quatrain 874]

There's no question that every tongue
is a curtain over the heart:
when the curtain is moved,
the mysteries hidden behind it reach us.
This small curtain, like a slice of roast meat,
conceals a hundred suns.

No matter what the words themselves are saying,
still the scent of the speaker speaks of truth or falsehood.
You can tell the difference
between the breeze that drifts from a garden
and the arid bluster from the ash heap.

The scents of truth and plausible falsehood
are apparent in the breath, like musk and garlic.
If you cannot distinguish sincerity from duplicity,
blame your own rotten sense of smell.
The voices of mercenaries and dedicated heros
are as distinct as the characteristics of the fox and the lion.

To say it another way, the tongue
is just like the lid of a cooking pot:
when it is opened you know what the food inside it is;
but one whose sense of smell is keen
can tell from the steam
whether it's a sour stew simmering
or a delicate dessert.

[*Mathnawi* VI: 4890–4898]

"Tell me truly, how can you know a person's hidden nature?"
"I sit beside him in silence
and make patience a ladder to climb upward:
patience is the key to success.
And if in his presence there should gush from my heart
words from beyond this realm of joy and sorrow,
I know that he has sent it to me from the depths of a soul
illumined like Canopus rising in Yemen."
The speech in my heart
comes from that auspicious neighborhood.
Surely, there is a window from heart to heart.

[*Mathnawi* VI: 4912–4916]

"THE NIGHT IS OVER, my friend, but our story has not yet ended." The night and darkness of this world may pass, but the light of these words shines brighter every moment. Even so did the night of the prophets' lives pass, but the light of their words has not yet ceased—nor will it ever.

[*Fihi ma Fihi*: Discourse 49]

BAHAEDDIN WELED (Sultan Weled) told us one day:

My father said, "O Bahaeddin, when the seed of my teaching has taken root in your heart, you will understand; reflect deeply on my teaching and really try to absorb it and if you do, felicity will be yours. Know that the body of the prophets, the saints and their friends will never perish. A seed thrown into the earth may appear to die and disappear; however, at the end of a few days, it comes to life and flowers. In a similar way the body of the prophets and the saints will also come to life again."

Mevlana was absorbed in the mystery described in the Qur'an [51:21]: *Have you not looked within?*

> There is nothing in the world
> that exists outside yourself;
> look into the depths of your being
> for that which you desire.

[*Menaqib al-Arifin:* 251]